A Phrasal Verb Affair

When John runs out on Maria
and runs off with another woman,
Maria tracks him down to do him in.

D1065979

Keith Kohnhorst

illustrations by Nancy Shrewsbury Nadel

PR••LINGUA
LEARNING

Pro Lingua Learning
PO Box 4467
Rockville, MD 20849
Office: 301-424-8900
Orders: 800-888-4741
Email: Info@ProLinguaLearning.com
Web: www.ProLinguaLearning.com

At Pro Lingua,
our objective is to foster an approach to learning and teaching
that we call **interplay**, *the* **inter***action of language learners and teachers*
with their materials, the language and culture, and each other
in active, creative, and productive **play**.

This book was edited by Raymond C. Clark, designed by Susannah Clark, and illustrated by Nancy Shrewsbury Nadel. It was set in Californian, and the title on the cover and title page is in Viner Hand ITC.

Copyright © 2003 by Keith Kohnhorst

ISBN: 978-0-86647-165-7

Acknowledgements

My thanks to Tom Scovel and Dr. Jain, professors at San Francisco State University,
and to John Fleming, chair of the ESL department at De Anza College,
for their inspiration and input,
and to my wife, Lisa, for putting upwith my phrasal verb obsession.

Keith Kohnhorst

ACKNOWLEDGEMENTS

My thanks to Dr. Tom Scovel and Dr. Jain, professors at San Francisco State University, and to John Fleming, chair of the ESL Department at De Anza College, for their inspiration and input, and to my wife, Lisa, for putting up with my phrasal verb obsession.

Keith Kohnhorst

TABLE OF CONTENTS

The Cast of Characters viii

A Brief Introduction to Phrasal Verbs 1

User's Guide 4

Scene 1: Building Up Anger 6

Scene 2: I Wish I Could Count On You 17

Scene 3: Fighting Off Something Worse than a Cold 26

Scene 4: I Gave In 36

Scene 5: You Two Will Iron Out Your Differences 45

Scene 6: She Has Trouble Holding Down a Job 56

Scene 7: You Let Us Down 65

Scene 8: I Opened Up to You 77

Scene 9: She Puts Me Down 88

Scene 10: I've Run Out of Patience 97

Scene 11: Stick Up for Yourself 107

Scene 12: I Need to Sort a Few Things Out 118

Scene 13: I Straightened Myself Out 127

Scene 14: I'm Going to Stand Out 138

Scene 15: My Love for Him Is All Used Up 147

Answer Key 157

Phrasal Verb Glossary 176

Reconstruction 183

Other Books of Interest from Pro Lingua 184

THE CAST OF CHARACTERS

Maria

John

Joan

Buddy

Bobbi

Elaine

Mr. Henson

Bartender

A Phrasal Verb Affair

A Brief Introduction to Phrasal Verbs

The Importance of Phrasal Verbs

Students need to master phrasal verbs to be proficient in English because native speakers use them all the time in both formal and informal writing and conversation. The number of phrasal verbs, like the world's population, keeps growing and growing. (*The Longman Dictionary of Phrasal Verbs* lists over 12,000 entries.) Monosyllabic verbs (e.g., take, put, buy) are continually joining with particles (e.g., in, out, on, off) to form new verbs (e.g., chill out, log on).

For most students of English, learning how to use phrasal verbs is a major challenge. Phrasal verbs occur in Germanic languages but very few others. They are semantically and grammatically complex. So it's no wonder that students avoid them, or why so many teachers and grammar books cover them in only a superficial way. This book will give students the foundation they need to develop an active understanding and use of phrasal verbs—and they'll have fun in the process.

Defining a Phrasal Verb

Just as phrasal verbs are difficult for ESL students to figure out, linguists have a hard time agreeing on what a phrasal verb is. Most grammarians define a phrasal verb as a verb followed by a particle (often called a preposition or an adverb). In some cases, the particle may be followed by a preposition, resulting in a three-word verb.

> He **put off** [postponed] his meeting.
> I **ran into** [met] an old friend yesterday.
> I can't **put up with** [tolerate] his behavior anymore.

Semantic Creativity

In his definitive work *The Phrasal Verb in English*, Dwight Bolinger called phrasal verbs "an outpouring of lexical creativeness that surpasses anything else in our language."

> 1. A war **broke out** [began].
> 2. The baseball player **broke out of** [ended] his hitting slump.
> 3. His face **broke out** [erupted] in red spots.
> 4. The prisoner **broke out** [escaped].
> 5. He **broke out** [opened] an expensive bottle of wine.

Semantic Complexity

A phrasal verb can have more than one meaning. For example: When Mary **put on** her wedding dress, we thought she had **put on** 25 pounds in the past month, but she had put a pillow under the dress and was **putting** us **on**.

put on clothes	**put on** weight	**putting** us **on**
literal/transparent	*figurative/semi-transparent*	*idiomatic/opaque*
concrete meaning	We can see the	It is difficult to
of direction and	relationship to	see the literal
position	literal meaning	meaning

Of course, the **literal** meaning is easiest for students to understand. The **figurative** meaning is harder, but we can see the relationship to the literal meaning. The **idiomatic** meaning can only be understood from the context of the entire sentence. This book focuses on phrasal verbs with figurative or idiomatic meanings (e.g., **put on** weight, **put** somebody **on**).

Grammatical Complexity
This book contains three types of phrasal verbs:

       1. verb + adverb, as in: The plane **took off** [departed].

       2. verb + preposition, as in: Don't **buy into** [believe] his argument.

       3. verb + adverb + preposition, as in: She **looks up to** [respects] her parents.

Verb + Adverb
Only verb + adverb combinations are separable.

       I **asked** Mary **out**.

       I **asked out** Mary.

Only verb + adverb combinations can be intransitive (not take an object).

       My car **broke down**.

Pronoun objects always come before the adverb.

       I can't **figure** it **out**.

Verb + Preposition
This book contains verb + preposition combinations that are figurative or idiomatic and thus seem to function as a semantic unit.

       He **looked into** the problem.

       She's **building on** her success.

Not included are verb + preposition combinations in which the meaning can be understood from the verb alone and is not figuratively extended.

       I can **depend on him**.

These examples can be identified as verb + preposition combinations because the verb and preposition cannot be separated (e.g. *He **looked** the problem **into**. She's ***building** her success **on**). Verb + preposition combinations are always transitive; the preposition always takes an object.

Verb + Adverb + Preposition
Again, these three-word verbs form a semantic unit. The three-word verb always takes an object, which always follows the preposition.

       My boss **looks down on** me.

       I'm **coming down with** a cold.

User's Guide

The Text

Each scene in the text follows the same sequence of activities. The title of the scene features a phrasal verb that is important to the story line. On the first page of each scene, there are questions to stimulate **discussion** in groups or pairs. In "Setting Up," the questions prepare the students for the events in the scene. In "Pair Up," the questions explore the meaning of the phrasal verb featured in the title.

The illustrations at the beginning of each scene can be used to prepare the students for the events in the scene. Students can simply describe the picture, or they can try to guess what will happen in the scene. This can be done in pairs or as an activity for the whole class.

The dialogue in the scene can be used in a variety of ways. One option is to play the corresponding track from the CD as the students **listen**. Then the students **read** the script individually or in small groups (the number in the group depending on the number of characters in the scene, always at least three, including a person who reads the introduction and other scene-setting lines). The use of the CD is, however, optional, and the class can work on the script by simply reading it through and then working on comprehension.

As the students work on the dialogue, the focus should be on understanding the events. This may generate questions about the meaning of the phrasal verbs and other **vocabulary** in the script. The teacher can circulate to clarify the meanings for the students.

The **exercises** following the scene are self-explanatory. They can be done individually, in pairs, or in groups according to the instructions. The purpose of the exercises is to explore the form, meaning, and usage of the phrasal verbs. There are more than 200 different verbs in the entire text.

The **answers** to the exercises are available for self-checking on pages 156–174. A glossary of all the phrasal verbs in this text is on pages 175–182 for reference.

A reconstruction of the entire story in pictures follows the glossary. It can be used as a summary activity.

The CD

The CD has two sections. In the first section (tracks 1–15), each scene is dramatically presented on a different track. In the second section (tracks 16–30), the phrasal verbs that occur in each scene are spoken in a phrase or sentence from that scene. These tracks can be used for pronunciation practice, for summarizing the scene, or for reviewing previous scenes.

SCENE 1: BUILDING UP ANGER

Setting Up Scene 1

In Scene 1, Maria and her husband, John, build up anger towards one another. How do couples build up anger toward one another? What might happen if their anger builds up too much?

Pair Up

With a classmate, discuss the following questions.

1. What are some good ways to build up your vocabulary?

2. If you feel anger building up against your friend, what do you do?

3. Would you like to build up your confidence to talk to Americans? How could you do this?

BUILDING UP ANGER

It's Tuesday morning, and John and Maria are having breakfast. Maria suspects that John was up to no good last night. A mix of fear and anger is building up inside her. John feels hungover.

Maria: John, I didn't want to bring this up. I know we've been trying to build on the trust we established in therapy, and I'm so happy that we've bounced back from a near divorce, but I smelled perfume on you last night that wasn't mine. Am I right?

John: (*Shouting*) I don't answer to anyone, especially to you and your accusations, which never add up to anything, anyway!

Maria: You don't have to blow up like that. It makes me think you're trying to brush me off because you feel guilty about something.

John: No, it's because you bring out the worst in me with your mistrust. You think I ask out every woman I see. Why don't you back up your accusations with some proof? Hire a detective or something.

Maria: You bring it on yourself by not talking to me. I'm your wife, for God's sake!

John: Yes, and a wife is supposed to believe in her husband!

John breaks off the argument by going into the bathroom and slamming the door. Maria breaks down, bursts into tears, and runs into the bedroom, fearing that she and John are going to break up.

A Phrasal Verb Affair

EXERCISES FOR SCENE 1

A. What's Going On?

Discuss the following questions with your classmates.

1. Why is Maria reluctant to bring up her worries?
2. What does John mean when he shouts, "I don't answer to anyone!"? Why does he shout?
3. What kind of proof would Maria need to back up her accusations?
4. What does John bring on himself, according to Maria?
5. Why does John feel that Maria brings out the worst in him? The worst what?
6. What do you think John was really up to last night?

Transitive or Intransitive?

Like one-word verbs, phrasal verbs are transitive or intransitive. The majority are transitive.

A **transitive** verb takes an object noun, which answers the questions "who" or "what."

> He **brought up** a good question.

"A good question," an object noun, answers the question, "What did he **bring up**?"

An **intransitive** verb does not take an object noun; the words that follow an intransitive verb do not answer the question "who" or "what."

> My car **broke down** yesterday.

Some verbs can be transitive or intransitive:

> (T) She is **building up** her confidence.

> (I) Her confidence is **building up**.

B. Search Out

Part 1

With a classmate, find and underline 16 phrasal verbs from Scene 1 that begin with the letters A or B and contain the following particles: in, into, out, up, down, on, off. The verbs are listed in Exercise D, but try to find them first.

Part 2

In the spaces below, list the phrasal verbs you have underlined. Write "T" next to each transitive verb and write its object. If the phrase includes a pronoun object, write the pronoun between the two parts of the verb. If the verb is intransitive, write "I" next to it. The first three are done for you.

1.	T	be (was) up to	no good
2.	I	build up	
3.	T	bring this up	
4.	___	_____	_____
5.	___	_____	_____
6.	___	_____	_____
7.	___	_____	_____
8.	___	_____	_____
9.	___	_____	_____
10.	___	_____	_____
11.	___	_____	_____
12.	___	_____	_____
13.	___	_____	_____
14.	___	_____	_____
15.	___	_____	_____
16.	___	_____	_____

C. Look Back

With a classmate, find two phrasal verbs in Scene 1 with the particles "back" and "to." Then write your own sentences using the phrasal verbs.

1. _____

_____

2. _____

_____

D. Match Up

Match the phrasal verb with the best definition and write the correct letter in the blank.

Part 1

1.	be up to	_____	a.	to have a particular result
2.	build up	_____	b.	to use something as a base for further development
3.	bring up	_____	c.	to rudely ignore someone or their ideas
4.	build on	_____	d.	to introduce a subject
5.	add up to	_____	e.	to yield or amount to
6.	blow up	_____	f.	to be doing something (often something bad)
7.	brush off	_____	g.	to increase gradually
8.	bring out	_____	h.	to explode with anger

Part 2

9.	ask out	_____	a.	to end an intimate relationship with someone
10.	back up	_____	b.	to erupt in (laughter, tears, applause, etc.)
11.	bring on	_____	c.	to have faith or trust in
12.	believe in	_____	d.	to suddenly end something
13.	break off	_____	e.	to lose control of your emotions
14.	break down	_____	f.	to cause something unpleasant to happen
15.	burst into	_____	g.	to invite someone on a date
16.	break up	_____	h.	to support what someone is saying

E. Talk It Over

Discuss the following questions with your classmates.

1. What have you been up to lately?
2. What ESL achievements or successes are you building on?
3. Whom have you brushed off lately? Why? Who has brushed you off lately? Why?
4. Who brings out the best in you? How do they do it?
5. What do you do when you feel a lot of stress building up?
6. Who or what makes you burst into laughter? Explain.

Most transitive two-word verbs are separable; this means that the noun can precede (example 1) or follow (example 2) the particle:

*(1) He **asked out** Mary.*

*(2) He **asked** Mary **out**.*

However, if the object is a pronoun, it must precede the particle.

*(1) He **asked** her **out**.*

*(2) *He **asked out** her.*

F. Split Up

Fill in the blanks with the correct phrasal verbs from the list below and insert the correct pronoun between the verb and particle. Some verbs require a change in tense.

bring on   brush off   back up   bring up   build up   ask out   bring out

1. What my father said was wrong, but please don't _____ at dinner.

2. Susie tried to talk to the boss about our complaints, but he _____.

3. Mary said that she wasn't drunk last night, and I can _____.

4. She has a great sense of humor, and her husband _____ in her.

5. He has a lot of problems, but he _____ himself by lying to people.

6. Enrique is attracted to Mayuki. He wants to _____.

7. Terry doesn't have much self-esteem, but his teacher is trying to

    _____ by praising his good work.

Phrasal verbs are easier to understand when the verb describes (1) a physical action:

> The prisoner was **tied up**.

or (2) the primary meaning of the word:

> Your numbers don't **add up**.

These verbs are **literal**.

Phrasal verbs are harder to understand when the verb describes an abstraction, which is not its ordinary meaning but has similar qualities:

> I was **tied up** in traffic. The person is not being tied up with rope, but since they are unable to move in traffic, the effect is somewhat similar.

> Your story doesn't **add up**. The details of the person's story do not ring true.

These types of verbs are **figurative**.

G. Literal or Figurative?

Fill in the blank with the correct phrasal verb from the list below. Some answers require an object pronoun or a change in tense. Write "F" if the verb is used figuratively and "L" if it's used literally.

bring up   add up to   build up   burst into   bring on   bring out   build on

_____ 1. We need more bricks to _____ the wall a few feet higher.

_____ 2. He has worked for a number of dot-com companies and has _____ an impressive resume.

_____ 3. You _____ your cold by not getting enough rest.

_____ 4. The man was bored with the magic act, so he shouted, "_____ the clowns!"

_____ 5. Boris and Tanya bought a cute little two-bedroom home. When they have a baby, Boris is going to _____ another room.

_____ 6. Son, you sold your first car today. You have reason to be proud. Now you have to _____ your first success until you've sold as many cars as I have.

_____ 7. All of his efforts to make her love him didn't _____ anything. She married someone else.

_____ 8. What do 3,150 + 2,264 + 1,601 _____ ?

_____ 9. Don't _____ Tuan's recent divorce when he visits.

_____ 10. The boxes in the basement were too heavy for Linda, so she had her son _____ to the kitchen.

_____ 11. When the match landed in the wastebasket, the papers inside it _____ flames.

_____ 12. After the pianist finished her virtuoso performance, the crowd _____ into applause.

_____ 13. Luis, will you get the lemonade and _____ to the patio?

_____ 14. That neighborhood boy who smokes and curses is going to _____ the worst in my son.

H. Check-Up

Work with a classmate to fill in the blanks. Some verbs require a change in tense. Then read the dialogue together.

Part 1

> build on   bring up   back up   bring on   add up to   bring out   believe in

Ricky and his mother are discussing his suspension from school for lying to the police.

Mother: Ricky, you (1)_____ your school suspension by (2)_____ Harry's lie about where he got the marijuana.

Ricky: (*Rebelliously*) Friends take care of friends.

Mother: (*Angrily*) Not when his story (3)_____ a big lie and gets you in trouble, too. I wish you'd never met him; he's a big troublemaker. He's (4)_____ a side of you that I didn't know existed—a deceitful side.

Ricky: (*Angrily*) I wish I had never (5)_____ any of this _____. I knew you'd be against me. You don't (6)_____ me. You think I'm a liar.

Mother: (*Sadly*) I suppose I do. Our relationship has been (7)_____ honesty and trust. I'm not so sure we have that anymore.

Part 2

> brush off   blow up   build up   break up   break off   be up to   ask out   break down

Alan meets his best friend, Tom, in the hallway of their college dormitory.

Alan: (*Excitedly*) Hey, Letty just (8)_____ with her boyfriend. They had been going out for three years.

Tom: What happened?

Alan: I guess he got angry and (9)_____ at her and told her he never
        wanted to see her again. Letty (10)_____ and cried when
        she told me about it. She didn't want to (11)_____ the relationship
        _____, but when she saw him yesterday, he was with another woman, and
        (12)_____ her _____ without saying a word.

Tom: (*Teasingly*) I know what you (13)_____. You're going to
        (14)_____ her _____. You've been wanting to date her for years.

Alan: (*Seriously*) She's not ready to date right now. Besides, we've been
        (15)_____ a close friendship for the last year. I don't want to ruin that.

I. Make It Up

With a classmate, write a short dialogue in which a student who has been building up a lot of anger
against her teacher has a confrontation with him about her poor essay grade. Use at least seven
phrasal verbs from Scene 1. When you're finished, read the dialogue to the class.

J. Sum Up and Look Ahead

Briefly summarize what happened in Scene 1. Then ask a classmate what they think will happen in
Scene 2 when John goes to check on Maria in the bedroom.

Scene 2: I Wish I Could Count On You

Setting Up Scene 2

Why does Maria feel she can't count on John to tell the truth? What might have happened in the past to make her feel this way?

Pair Up

Discuss the following questions with a classmate.

1. In the following situation, who is talking to whom, and where is this happening?
   "You can count on me to be here every day on time, to answer any questions you might have, and to give a lot of homework. Can I count on you to be here every day on time, to answer any questions I might ask, and to do a lot of homework?"

2. Can you count on the following people or government agencies? Why or why not? What can you count on or not count on them to do for you?
   A stranger?
   Your family?
   The police?
   Your employer?
   The Internal Revenue Service?
   A car salesman?

I Wish I Could Count On You

Five minutes later, John goes to check on Maria in the bedroom.

John: (*Softly*) Please don't cry, Maria. Let me clear up any doubts you might have about last night. I stayed late at work because my sales haven't been very good lately and I need to work harder or I won't get a Christmas bonus. Anyway, Buddy was there catching up on some accounts he's fallen behind on, and he came up with the idea of going out for a drink. I told him I felt like I was coming down with a cold, but you know how pushy he is. I said I would go, but that I was trying to clean up my act by cutting down on alcohol and would only have one beer. Anyway, at the bar I was minding my own business when some woman came on to me. She was drunk and loud, and I tried to brush her off, but she wouldn't leave me alone until I danced with her.

Maria: (*Angry and surprised*) You expect me to buy into this story?

John: (*Frustrated*) Calm down, Maria. I wasn't attracted to her at all. Please believe me, because it's true—and Buddy will back up everything I've said!

Maria: (*Sarcastic*) I'm sure he will. He always bails you out when you need an alibi.

John: I'm telling you, nothing happened. Don't let this come between us.

Maria: (*Sadly*) I wish I could believe you, but I don't. When things like this come up, I feel like I can't count on you to tell the truth. After all, you said you weren't attracted to Melissa, either.

John: (*Angrily*) Stop it, Maria, will you? Why are you bringing Melissa into the conversation?

Maria: (*Shouting*) You're the one who needs to stop it!

John marches out of the room and slams the door. Maria beats on her pillow.

EXERCISES FOR SCENE 2

A. What's Going On?
Discuss the following questions with your classmates.

1. Why do you think John went to check on Maria?
2. What "act" is John trying to clean up?
3. John said a woman came on to him. How might a woman come on to a man? How might a man come on to a woman?
4. Do you believe John's story about what happened at the bar? Why or why not?
5. Why do you think John told Maria that he danced with another woman?
6. Why does Maria say "I'm sure he will" sarcastically?
7. Who do you think Melissa is? Why does John get angry when Maria brings Melissa into the conversation?

B. Search Out
Part 1
With a classmate, find and underline 14 phrasal verbs from Scene 2 that begin with the letters B or C and contain the following particles: in, into, out, up, down, on, off. The verbs are listed in Exercise D, but try to find them first. Note: Do not include "brush off" or "back up"; they appeared in Scene 1.

Part 2
In the spaces on the next page, list all the phrasal verbs you have underlined. Write "T" next to each transitive verb and write its object. If the phrase includes a pronoun object, write the pronoun between the two parts of the verb. Note that if the phrase is a three-word verb, the pronoun comes after the verb. Also note that "count on" is a verb + preposition, and the pronoun follows the preposition. If the verb is intransitive, write "I" next to it.

1. ___ _____ _____
2. ___ _____ _____
3. ___ _____ _____
4. ___ _____ _____
5. ___ _____ _____
6. ___ _____ _____
7. ___ _____ _____
8. ___ _____ _____
9. ___ _____ _____
10. ___ _____ _____
11. ___ _____ _____
12. ___ _____ _____
13. ___ _____ _____
14. ___ _____ _____

C. Look Back

With a classmate, find two phrasal verbs from Scene 2 with the particles "between" and "behind." Then write your own sentences using the phrasal verbs.

1. _____

_____

2. _____

_____

D. Match Up

Match the phrasal verb with the best definition and write the correct letter in the blank.

Part 1

1. check on	_____	a. to think of an idea or plan
2. clear up	_____	b. to make someone or something become moral or responsible
3. catch up on	_____	c. to find out how or what someone is doing
4. come up with	_____	d. to help someone understand the facts of a situation
5. come down with	_____	e. to reduce the amount of something
6. clean up	_____	f. to do work one should have done earlier
7. cut down on	_____	g. to become ill

Part 2

8. come on to	_____	a. to believe an idea, often a false one
9. calm down	_____	b. to depend on or be certain of someone or something
10. bail out	_____	c. to arise
11. buy into	_____	d. to help someone out of a difficult situation
12. come up	_____	e. to make clear that one is interested in someone
13. count on	_____	f. to become relaxed after being nervous or excited
14. bring into	_____	g. to introduce someone or something into a discussion

E. Talk It Over
Discuss the following questions with your classmates.

1. What work have you fallen behind on and need to catch up on?
2. What do you need to cut down on?
3. What do you do or take when you come down with something?
4. What stereotypes about America or Americans do foreigners buy into before they come to the United States? What stereotypes did you buy into? Were they true?
5. Whom or what do you count on?
6. Have you ever bailed a friend out of a difficult situation? Has a friend bailed you out? Explain.

F. Split Up
Fill in the blanks with the correct phrasal verbs from the list below and insert the correct pronoun between the verb and particle. Some verbs require a change in tense.

calm down   bail out   bring into   clear up   clean up

1. My teacher and I had a misunderstanding in class, but we _____ in her office.
2. My friend keeps asking me to give him the homework answers, but I told him I can't _____ any longer. He needs to do his own work.
3. When she heard that the right-wing candidate was going to be president, she began to cry, so we had to _____.
4. My teacher said my essay had too many grammar errors and that I needed to _____ before she would accept it.
5. Helene's family doesn't like to talk about Jim, so don't _____ the conversation.

G. Literal or Figurative?

Fill in the blank with the correct phrasal verb from the list below. Some answers require an object pronoun or a change in tense. Write "F" if the verb is used figuratively and "L" if it's used literally.

clear up   count on   bring into   bail out   come up   buy into   catch up

____ 1. Did you hear that the newspaper tycoon is going to _____ a satellite TV company?

____ 2. When I first moved to the United States, I _____ the American dream—you know a house, two cars—but three years later, I'm still struggling to support my family and pay the rent.

____ 3 I heard on the weather report that it's going to _____ tomorrow and be a beautiful day.

____ 4. Students, I know you're confused about what's going to be on the midterm, so let me take a few minutes to _____ things _____.

____ 5. Tuyet, please go out to the garage and find the Christmas lights and _____ them _____ the house.

____ 6. Jim: Larry, tell Tina that I wasn't coming on to her sister at the party.
Tina: Don't _____ Larry _____ this! This is our problem.

____ 7. My aunt lives down in Florida, but she'll be _____ to Maine to visit me soon.

____ 8. Every time I'm ready to take a vacation something always _____— one of my kids gets sick, my car breaks down, or work piles up.

____ 9. My daughter is just learning to add, so she still _____ her fingers.

____ 10. Dieter, you didn't clean up the house like you promised. I _____ you, and you let me down.

____ 11. In the Boston Marathon, the Kenyan runner tripped and fell and couldn't _____.

____ 12. Simon, you've missed five classes and two assignments. It's going to be difficult for you to _____.

_____13. Lisa, I can't keep _____ by telling Harry that you're having lunch. Sooner or later, he's going to find out that you're meeting Tim at the park.

_____14. My brother was arrested for drinking and driving, and I had to pay $1,000 to _____.

H. Finish Up

Work with a classmate and complete these sentences with your own clauses.

1. When my boss came on to me at work, _____
2. I've got some work I need to catch up on, so _____
3. I'm trying to cut down on fatty foods because _____
4. If you come up with the answer, _____
5. Whenever I think I'm coming down with a cold, _____
6. He tried to clear up the misunderstanding, but _____
7. You can buy into your feelings that you're a bad person or _____
8. Parents should check on their children since _____
9. I tried to calm her down, but _____
10. If sad memories come up, _____

I. Make It Up

With a classmate, write a short dialogue in which you confront a friend whom you had counted on to turn in your midterm essay while you were sick, but who ended up losing it. Use at least seven phrasal verbs from Scene 2. When you're finished, read the dialogue to the class.

J. Sum Up and Look Ahead

Briefly summarize what happened in Scene 2. Then ask a classmate what advice Maria's best friend, Joan, will give her about her relationship with John in Scene 3.

Scene 3: Fighting Off Something Worse Than a Cold

Setting Up Scene 3

In Scene 3 Maria says she's fighting off a cold, but her best friend, Joan, says she looks like she's fighting off something worse than a cold. What does Joan mean?

Pair Up

Discuss the following questions with a classmate.

1. In the United States, some of the more common ways people try to fight off a cold are to take medicine or Vitamin C and get more sleep. Some people are now using herbs to fight off colds. Do you know what some of these herbs are? Do you think they're effective?
2. What do you think are some of the best ways to fight off a cold? What do people in your home country do to fight off a cold?
3. People fight off other things besides colds. Can you think of a few? As a student, you've probably had to fight off the desire to stop doing your homework and, instead, watch TV or go online. Do you usually fight off these feelings, or do you give in to them? What do you do or tell yourself to fight them off?

FIGHTING OFF SOMETHING WORSE THAN A COLD

It's Tuesday afternoon, and Maria and her co-worker and best friend, Joan, are having lunch together in a café.

Joan: I'm buying. Anything you want.

Maria: Thanks, Joan, but I'm not hungry.

Joan: What's wrong? You look so pale.

Maria: I'm fighting off a cold.

Joan: You look like you're fighting off something worse than a cold.

Maria: (*Sighs sadly*) I guess I am, but I don't want to dump on you and drag you into this mess.

Joan: That's what friends are for. Go ahead. Fill me in on what John's been up to.

Maria: Maybe I'm dreaming the whole thing up, but I'm worried John is having another affair. He danced with some woman at a bar last night. He didn't come home until 2:00. He said it was no big deal, that she forced herself on him, and that I'm distrustful. Maybe I do dwell on the negative too much.

Joan: (*Incredulous*) He said you're distrustful? Boy, he can really dish it out, but he sure can't take it.

Maria: At least I didn't have to force it out of him. He told me himself.

Joan: And that makes it okay?

Maria: No, but ...

Joan: (*Takes Maria's hands in hers*) Maria, I feel for you. You're scared your marriage is going to fall apart again and end in divorce this time, so you don't want to face up to the fact that John's the cheating type. But I don't want you to end up getting hurt again. You need to figure out what to do.

Maria: You're right. (*Nervously changing the subject*) Oh, gosh! Look at the time! I wish I didn't have to go back to work. I just don't feel up to it today.

Joan: Why don't you take the afternoon off? I'll fill in for you and finish up.

Maria: Joan, you're a saint. What would I do without you?

EXERCISES FOR SCENE 3

A. What's Going On?

Discuss the following questions with your classmates.

1. What are friends for, according to Joan?
2. How does Joan know that Maria is upset because of John?
3. What does Joan "feel for" Maria?
4. Do you think Joan is right when she says Maria doesn't want to face up to the fact that John's the cheating type? Explain.
5. Why does Maria nervously change the subject after Joan's heart-to-heart talk?
6. Is Joan a good friend to Maria? Why or why not?

B. Search Out

Part 1

With a classmate, find and underline 16 phrasal verbs from Scene 3 that begin with the letters D, E, or F and contain the following particles: in, into, out, up, down, on, off. The verbs are listed in Exercise D, but try to find them first.

Part 2

In the spaces on the next page, list all the phrasal verbs you have underlined. Write "T" for each transitive verb and write its object. If the phrase includes a pronoun object, write the pronoun between the two parts of the verb. If the verb is intransitive, write "I" next to it.

1. ___ _____ _____
2. ___ _____ _____
3. ___ _____ _____
4. ___ _____ _____
5. ___ _____ _____
6. ___ _____ _____
7. ___ _____ _____
8. ___ _____ _____
9. ___ _____ _____
10. ___ _____ _____
11. ___ _____ _____
12. ___ _____ _____
13. ___ _____ _____
14. ___ _____ _____
15. ___ _____ _____
16. ___ _____ _____

C. Look Back

With a classmate, find two phrasal verbs in Scene 3 with the particles " for" and "apart." Then write your own sentences using the phrasal verbs.

1. _____

_____

2. _____

_____

D. Match Up

Match the phrasal verb with the best definition and write the correct letter in the blank.

Part 1

1. fight off _____
2. dump on _____
3. drag into _____
4. fill in _____
5. dream up _____
6. force on _____
7. dwell on _____
8. dish out _____

a. to tell someone about recent events they're unaware of
b. to think of a plan or idea, especially an unusual one
c. to tell someone all of your problems
d. to make someone get involved even if they don't want to
e. to give freely
f. to think or talk about something unpleasant for too long
g. to try hard to repel or keep away
h. to push on someone something that they don't want

Part 2

9. force out of _____
10. end in _____
11. face up to _____
12. end up _____
13. figure out _____
14. feel up to _____
15. fill in for _____
16. finish up _____

a. to feel capable or well enough to do something
b. to think about something until you understand it
c. to complete a task
d. to do someone's work
e. to come to be in a particular situation without planning it
f. to make someone tell you something
g. to accept or acknowledge an unpleasant fact or situation
h. to result in

E. Talk It Over

Discuss the following questions with your classmates.

1. Who has dumped on you lately? Why?
2. What unpleasant situation have you been dragged into lately?
3. What problems did you dwell on when you first came to the United States? Do you dwell on the same problems or different ones now?
4. How do adults force information out of children?
5. What do you do when you don't feel up to going to work? cooking dinner? doing homework?
6. What kind of excuses do students give when they haven't done their homework?
7. What facts don't people like to face up to?

F. Split Up

Fill in the blanks with the correct phrasal verbs from the list below and insert the correct pronoun between the verb and particle. Some verbs require a change in tense.

dream up   finish up   figure out   dish out   fight off   fill in   force out of

1. Rafael won't admit that he stole the money out of my wallet, so I'm going to have to _____ him.

2. I've never seen the boss yell at so many people. When he's angry he can sure

   _____.

3. Ahmed flirts with me one day, and then he ignores me the next. I can't

   _____.

4. Boris says he saw a man last night prowling in our back yard, but I think he's

   _____. You know how wild children's imagination can be.

5. I feel like I'm coming down with something, so I'm taking large doses of vitamin C to _____.

6. When the owner returned from vacation, she called her assistant in to

   _____ on the latest news.

7. Your essay is good but incomplete; you need to _____ by writing a conclusion.

G. Literal or Figurative?

Fill in the blank with the correct phrasal verb from the list below. Some answers require an object pronoun or a change in tense. Write "F" if the verb is used figuratively and "L" if it's used literally.

dump on   drag into   face up to   dish out   fill in   end up   fight off   force out of

____ 1. He put his _____ the mirror to check his wrinkles.

____ 2. I know you miss Indira, but it's been four months since she left you. You need
to _____ the fact that she's not coming back.

____ 3. The government had better _____ that pothole on Highway 17,
or someone's going to get in an accident.

____ 4. I was going to be the group leader in class tomorrow, but I've come down with
the flu. Will you please _____ for me?

____ 5. Will you _____ the potatoes while I pour the wine?

____ 6. My husband called me every nasty name imaginable. He can really
_____ the abuse when he's upset.

____ 7. When Jorge swallowed a chicken bone and began to choke, Luis had to
_____ him by using the Heimlich maneuver.

____ 8 He wouldn't confess to the crime, so the detective tried to _____
it _____ him by threatening to lock him up.

____ 9. When the movie star left the hotel, his bodyguards had to _____
the fans who wanted to get an autograph.

___10. When I got a D on an essay I worked really hard on, I had to _____
the urge to cry.

___11. I always meet people who want to _____ all their problems _____
me by the end of our first date. Isn't there anyone who just wants to have fun?

____ 12. I get angry when I see that people _____ their trash _____ other
people's property.

____ 13. If you keep drinking, gambling, and smoking, you're going to
_____ six feet under before you're 50 years old.

___ 14. We were trying to get to Chestnut Street, but we _____ on a dead-end street.

___ 15. Our dog _____ a huge stick _____ the front yard.

___ 16. My friend is trying to _____ me _____ going to his mother's house instead of the ball game, but I won't let him.

H. Make It Up

With a classmate, write a dialogue in which you give advice to a friend who is trying to fight off the fear that her relationship is falling apart. Use at least eight phrasal verbs from Scene 3. When you're finished, read the dialogue to the class.

I. Sum Up and Look Ahead

Briefly summarize what happened in Scene 3. In Scene 4, John meets his co-worker, Buddy, in the break room. What will John and Buddy talk about?

Scene 4: I Gave In

Setting Up Scene 4

In Scene 4, John tells his co-worker, Buddy, that he gave in and told Maria part of the truth about what happened at the bar. Why do you think he gave in? What part of the truth do you think he told her, and what part didn't he tell her?

Pair Up

Read the following scene and discuss the questions with a classmate.

Teacher: (*Before taking attendance on the first day of class*) I'm only allowing 25 students, and the class is full, so if you're on the waiting list, you need to leave.

Student: Will you please add me? I've been trying to get in this class for two years.

Teacher: You're on the waiting list. Sorry.

Student: I know, but I'm a good student. I work two jobs and this is the only class I can take. Please?

Teacher: I shouldn't, but OK, I'll let you in.

1. Why did the teacher give in and let the student in?
2. Should the teacher have given in? Why or why not?
3. Have you had a teacher who has given in to you for something you wanted?
4. Tell each other about a situation in which you gave in.

I Gave In

It's Tuesday afternoon. John and Buddy meet in the break room at work.

John: Hey, what's going on?

Buddy: Not much. (*Pause*) You look terrible. What time did you get in last night?

John: Around 2:00.

Buddy: (*Smiling, teasingly*) So did you get away with your little fling, or did Maria find out?

John: Well, Maria freaked out when I told her that I danced with that woman Elaine at the bar.

Buddy: (*Surprised*) You told her? Why? What got into you?

John: I don't know. She was asking me all these questions, and I wanted to get her off my back, so I gave in. There was no getting around it. I had to tell her the truth.

Buddy: The whole truth?

John: No, Maria doesn't need to know the whole truth. What she doesn't know can't hurt her. And I'm sure she's already told her best friend, Joan, what I said. The last thing I need is the two of them ganging up on me.

Buddy: What is the whole truth, by the way?

John: (*Annoyed*) I don't want to go into it. It's none of your business.

Buddy: OK, OK. (*Pause*) Are you going to go out with Elaine again?

John: I don't know.

Exercises for Scene 4

A. What's Going On?

Discuss the following questions with your classmates.

1. Do you think John got away with his "little fling"? Why or why not?
2. Why is Buddy surprised that John told Maria that he danced with another woman?
3. What does John mean when he says, "What [Maria] doesn't know can't hurt her"? Do you agree? Explain.
4. How might Maria and Joan gang up on John?
5. What kind of relationship do John and Buddy have? How would you compare it to Maria and Joan's relationship?

B. Search Out

Part 1

With a classmate, find and underline ten phrasal verbs from Scene 4 that begin with the letters F or G and contain the following particles: in, into, out, up, down, on, off. The verbs are listed in Exercise D, but try to find them first.

Part 2

In the spaces on the next page, list all the phrasal verbs you have underlined. Write "T" next to each transitive verb and write its object. If the phrase includes a pronoun object, write the pronoun between the two parts of the verb. If the verb is intransitive, write "I" next to it.

1. ___ _____ _____
2. ___ _____ _____
3. ___ _____ _____
4. ___ _____ _____
5. ___ _____ _____
6. ___ _____ _____
7. ___ _____ _____
8. ___ _____ _____
9. ___ _____ _____
10. ___ _____ _____

C. Look Back

With a classmate, find two phrasal verbs in Scene 4 with the particles "away" and "around." Then write your own sentences using the phrasal verbs.

1. _____

_____

2. _____

_____

D. Match Up
Match the phrasal verb with the best definition and write the correct letter in the blank.

1. go on   _____   a. to become very excited or upset

2. get in   _____   b. to happen or take place

3. find out   _____   c. to surrender or yield

4. freak out   _____   d. to date someone

5. get into   _____   e. to discover or obtain information

6. get off __ back _____   f. to arrive

7. give in   _____   g. to join or work with others against someone

8. gang up on   _____   h. to negatively affect someone's behavior

9. go into   _____   i. to make someone stop annoying or bothering
                               someone

10. go out with   _____   j. to explain or discuss in detail

E. Talk It Over
Discuss the following questions with your classmates.

1. If you asked your child to come home before midnight but they didn't get in until 2:00 a.m., what would you do? Would you treat a girl differently from a boy?
2. How do you get someone off your back? Give an example.
3. Do you give in easily? to your spouse or partner? your boss? your parents? your children? salespeople?
4. At what age would you allow your children to go out with someone? the same age for a boy or girl?
5. What are some topics you'd rather not go into with people you don't know well or trust?
6. What would you do if you found out you had won the lottery? How would you spend your money? Would you quit school or your job?

F. Finish Up

Choose the correct phrasal verbs from the list below and add your own words to make the sentences complete.

get in	freak out	get into	give in	gang up on	go into
	find out		go out with		

1. It's a private matter. I don't _____.

2. Jimmy's so handsome. I'd love _____.

3. I spoil my kids rotten. "I want candy! I want a new toy!" they scream. I should say no, but _____.

4. When my dad _____ I had wrecked his car, _____.

5. I was at this wild party. I _____ until 4:00 a.m.

6. My son has never hit another child before. He's usually so gentle; I don't know _____. The other kids must have been _____, or he wouldn't have done it.

G. Check-Up

Work with a classmate to fill in the blanks. Some verbs require an object pronoun or a change in tense. Then read the dialogue together.

find out   get into   go into   freak out   give in   get off __ back

get in   go out with   gang up on   go on

Clara, age 17, tries to sneak quietly into her bedroom, but her father hears her and confronts her in the hallway.

Father: (*Angrily*) Are you just (1)_____? Do you know what time it is? Why are you home so late? What's (2)_____, young lady? I want the truth!

Clara: (*Sleepily*) Dad, I'm tired. Let's talk about it in the morning. I don't want to (3) _____ it right now.

Father: (*Shocked*) Oh, my God! What is that on your nose?

Clara: Calm down. Don't (4)_____. All of my friends have nose rings.

Father: Nose rings? What (5)_____ you to do something stupid like that? If all your friends jumped off the Golden Gate Bridge, would you jump, too?

Clara: If you keep hassling me, I might.

Father: (*Ignores her response and calls to his wife*) Honey! Clara's got something to show you!

Mother: (*Comes into the hall and sees the nose ring*) Oh, Clara! Why? You had such a pretty nose!

Clara: (*Begins to cry*) Why are you two (6)_____ me? I'm almost 18. I can do what I want. Will you (7)_____ and leave me alone?

Father: As long as you live in this house, you'll live by our rules. And I don't want you to (8)_____ Robert again.

Clara: (*Surprised*) How did you (9)_____ I was with Robert?

Father: I have my ways. (*Clara begins to cry again.*) You can cry all you want, but I'm not going to (10)_____ and change my mind.

H. Make It Up

With a classmate, write a brief dialogue about someone who wins the lottery and has to deal with the problems that come with becoming an instant millionaire. Use six phrasal verbs from Scene 4. When you're finished, read the dialogue to the class.

I. Sum Up and Look Ahead

Briefly summarize what happened in Scene 4. Then predict what John and Buddy will talk about in Scene 5. John ends Scene 5 by calling Buddy a jerk. What might Buddy say or do to anger John?

Scene 5: You Two Will Iron Out Your Differences

Setting Up Scene 5

In Scene 5, Buddy says to John, "You two will iron out your differences." Why? What do you think Buddy and John are talking about?

Pair Up

Take turns being a marriage counselor and give advice to a couple that wants to iron out their differences.

Problem 1

Wife:	You love the remote control more than you love me.
Husband:	Can't I relax for a few hours and watch TV?

Problem 2

Husband:	My sick mother should come and live with us.
Wife:	No, she hates me, and I'll be the one who takes care of her.

Problem 3

Wife:	You never talk to me about your feelings.
Husband:	What do you want me to say?

YOU TWO WILL IRON OUT YOUR DIFFERENCES

Buddy and John eat their lunches in silence. John eats only half his sandwich.

Buddy: What's wrong? Why aren't you eating?

John: (*Thoughtfully, sounding defeated*) Life is getting me down. Sometimes I feel like giving up and going off to some deserted island where there are no women and I can't get into trouble. Maria didn't use to be so possessive and jealous. She's not the same woman I fell in love with five years ago.

Buddy: Five years is a long time.

John: (*Ignoring Buddy's comment*) But I'm the one who fouled up and slept with Melissa. I guess I need to grow up and become a one-woman man and get on with my life. I'm 28 years old! When am I going to grow out of my adolescent ways? I can't go on this way. The only thing I'm going to get out of another affair is a big headache.

Buddy: Hang in there, pal. Maria'll get over it. You two will iron out your differences and get through this. (*Pause. Jokingly*) Listen, if you're going to become a one-woman man, how about fixing me up with woman number two, so I can go out with her? Maybe we'll hit it off and she'll forget about you and you'll be free of your problem.

John: Buddy, don't be a jerk.

Buddy: I was just joking.

EXERCISES FOR SCENE 5

A. What's Going On?
Discuss the following questions with your classmates.

1. Why does John feel like giving up? What does he feel like giving up?
2. According to John, how has Maria changed?
3. If John really decided to get on with his life, what should he do?
4. Has your opinion of John changed now that he has admitted he fouled up? Explain.
5. What adolescent ways does John need to grow out of?
6. John realizes that the only thing he'll get out of another affair is a big headache. Do you think he'll end the affair?
7. If John decides to give up Elaine, will he fix Buddy up with her?

B. Search Out
Part 1
With a classmate, find and underline 13 phrasal verbs from Scene 5 that begin with the letters F, G, H, or I and contain the following particles: in, into, out, up, down, on, off. The verbs are listed in Exercise D, but try to find them first.

Part 2
In the spaces on the next page, list all the phrasal verbs you have underlined. Write "T" next to each transitive verb and write its object. If the phrase includes a pronoun object, write the pronoun between the two parts of the verb. If the verb is intransitive, write "I" next to it.

1. ___ _____ _____
2. ___ _____ _____
3. ___ _____ _____
4. ___ _____ _____
5. ___ _____ _____
6. ___ _____ _____
7. ___ _____ _____
8. ___ _____ _____
9. ___ _____ _____
10. ___ _____ _____
11. ___ _____ _____
12. ___ _____ _____
13. ___ _____ _____

C. Look Back

With a classmate, find two phrasal verbs in Scene 5 with the particles "over" and "through." Then write your own sentences using the phrasal verbs.

1. _____
   _____

2. _____
   _____

D. Match Up

Match the phrasal verb with the best definition and write the correct letter in the blank.

Part 1

1. get _ down _____
2. give up _____
3. go off _____
4. foul up _____
5. grow up _____
6. get on with _____
7. grow out of _____

a. to continue or advance, often after an interruption
b. to leave, often suddenly
c. to make someone feel unhappy
d. to make a mistake or spoil something
e. to mature and stop a past behavior
f. to stop acting immature
g. to stop doing, having, or working on something

Part 2

8. go on _____
9. get out of _____
10. hang in _____
11. iron out _____
12. fix up _____
13. hit it off _____

a. to arrange for two people to meet, usually on a date
b. to obtain something beneficial from something or someone
c. to continue as before
d. to get along well with someone one just met
e. to persevere despite difficulties
f. to solve a problem or difficulty

E. Talk It Over

Discuss the following questions with your classmates.

1. What kind of people do you hit it off with?
2. What bad habits are you trying to give up?
3. How do you iron out your problems with people?
4. Has a friend or family member ever fixed you up? What happened?
5. Are you getting anything out of this book? Explain.
6. What do you do to cheer up a friend when life is getting them down?

F. Split Up
Fill in the blanks with the correct phrasal verbs from the list below and insert the correct pronoun between the verb and particle. Some verbs require a change in tense.

foul up   fix up   give up   iron out   get __ down

1. You know that gorgeous man who works with Sally? I'm going to ask her to
   _____ with him.
2. Seeing his old girlfriend kissing another guy really _____.
3. We used to have a lot of differences of opinion, but now that we've been married
   for five years, we've _____.
4. I was lost so I pulled into a gas station, but the guy _____ by
   giving me the wrong directions.
5. I used to smoke three packs of cigarettes a day, but I _____ when
   my kids started getting sick a lot.

G. Literal or Figurative?

Fill in the blank with the correct phrasal verb from the list below. Some answers require an object pronoun or a change in tense. Write "F" if the verb is used figuratively and "L" if it's used literally.

grow out of   grow up   go off   hit it off   iron out   get out of   go on

___ 1. Sally didn't think she would like my brother, but when they finally met, they really _____.

___ 2. The Mariners won the ball game when Ichiro _____ the wall.

___ 3. I am going to _____ a long walk.

___ 4. If you don't marry me, I won't be able to _____ living.

___ 5. If a man and woman have any major religious or philosophical differences, they should _____ before they marry.

___ 6. If you don't _____ those wrinkles now, your shirt will look terrible.

___ 7. Children _____ so quickly; enjoy them while you can.

___ 8. Your behavior at the party last night was just appalling. You really need to _____.

___ 9. **Rita:** My daughter has become so rebellious and negative.

Serena: Don't worry. That happens to a lot of teenagers. She'll _____ it.

___ 10. That shirt is way too small for him. He's _____ it.

___ 11. The surgery took over five hours, but the doctors finally _____ the tumor _____ him.

___ 12. That was the best ESL class I've ever taken. I _____ so much _____ it.

___ 13. You work 14-hour days; you don't exercise; you rarely see your kids. You can't _____ like this. You're going to have a heart attack.

___ 14. I know we're lost, but I think I know the street I'm on now. Let's _____ a little farther.

H. Fill In

Fill in the blanks with the correct phrasal verb from the list below. Some verbs require an object pronoun or a change in tense.

give up	go off	get ___ down	foul up	grow up	go on
hit it off	get on with	get out of	hang in	iron out	fix up
		grow out of			

1. You're 28. You need to move out of your parents' house and get a job. It's time to _____.

2. You and Tim should go and see my therapist. She's great. She'll help you two _____ your differences.

3. Cindy, you need to forget him and _____ your life. He's with someone else now.

4. Usually when I allow my friends to _____, my dates are a disaster, but this time my date and I _____.

5. **Troy:**   Hey, Phuong, did you go to the lecture on the global economy?

   Phuong: No. How was it? Did you _____ anything _____ it, or was it a waste of time?

6. My parents taught to me keep on trying and never _____.

7. **Nora:** The D I got on the midterm is _____. I studied so hard. I did well on the multiple choice, but I must have _____ on the essay question.

   Hazel: _____ there, Nora. You'll do better on the final.

8. It's going to be sad to see my grandmother _____ to a nursing home, but she needs full-time care now, and we can't _____ taking care of her.

9. Kids always go through a period when they try cigarettes. But don't worry, your daughter will _____.

I. Check-Up

Work with a classmate to fill in the blanks. Some verbs require an object pronoun or a change in tense. Then read the dialogue together.

Part 1

get on with   go on   go off   grow up   get out of   get __ down

Father: This house sure will be empty without Josh. The idea of him leaving and (1)_____ to college Monday is starting to (2)_____. To me, he's still a kid. I'm not sure he's mature enough to live away from home. I feel like he still has some (3)_____ to do.

Mother: I'll miss him too, but he'll (4)_____ a lot _____ living with other boys on campus. We can't (5)_____ holding his hand forever. It's time for him to (6)_____ his life and become a man.

Part 2

hang in   foul up   hit it off   grow out of   iron out   fix up   give up

Father: Is he still mad at me for (7)_____ with the Winslow girl down the street? They're both going to the same college, and she's so interesting. I thought they were a good match and would (8)_____.

Mother: You need to let go and (9)_____ the idea that you can control his life. He's (10)_____ being chaperoned on dates. He's almost 19, for heaven's sake! You (11)_____ and made a mistake, but there is still time to talk with him and (12)_____ things _____ before he leaves. (*Father begins to cry on his wife's shoulder, and she comforts him.*) (13)_____ there. Everything's going to be fine.

J. Make It Up

With a classmate, write a short dialogue between a brother and a sister. The sister is 22 and the brother is 18. The brother is angry that his parents won't let him go out with Heather; they want him to go out with a girl from church. The brother asks his sister how he can iron out his problem. Use eight phrasal verbs from Scene 5. When you're finished, read the dialogue to the class.

K. Sum Up and Look Ahead

Briefly summarize what happened in Scene 5. At the end of Scene 6, Maria calls her co-worker, Bobbi, "a lying gossip." Why do you think Maria says this?

Scene 6: She Has Trouble Holding Down a Job

Setting Up Scene 6

One of Maria's co-workers, Bobbi, has trouble holding down a job. What do you think "holding down a job" means? Why do you think Bobbi has trouble holding down a job?

Pair Up

Get together with a classmate and talk about the jobs you have held down. What were they? How long did you hold them down?

SHE HAS TROUBLE HOLDING DOWN A JOB

One day after John and Maria's blowup, Maria is arguing with a customer over the phone when a co-worker, Bobbi, comes into her office. Bobbi has had problems holding down a job because she would rather gossip than work.

Bobbi: Guess what, Maria?

Maria: (*Covers the phone*) Hold on, Bobbi. I'm talking to a customer. (*Bobbi sits down and begins tapping her pen on Maria's desk. To Bobbi*) Will you knock it off? (*Embarrassed that the customer thought Maria was talking to her*) Oh, not you, ma'am; there's someone here in my office. Yes, it's our fault that your electricity went out for six hours. No, we cannot refund your entire bill for the month, but you'll be receiving a partial refund shortly. (*Customer begins to argue*) Will you hear me out? (*Exasperated*) No, I am not going to hold up your refund, ma'am. In fact, I'll see to it that it's in the mail tomorrow. (*Angry*) Ma'am, if you keep it up, I'll have to hang up. (*Slams down the phone. To Bobbi*) I'm tired of kissing up to rude customers. They lash out at me with such anger. I used to be able to laugh it off. Now I have it out with them.

Bobbi: Did you have it out with John Monday night?

Maria: What are you talking about?

Bobbi: Guess who I saw hanging out with a young redhead at a bar that night?

Maria: My husband?

Bobbi: It's none of my business. That's why I've tried to hold off telling you. I really should keep out of other people's affairs. (*She starts to leave, but stops at the door.*) It was nothing really, if you consider dancing and kissing nothing. John couldn't keep his hands off her. Things were really heating up when they left together.

Maria: (*Tries to fight back her tears and anger but can't*) You're lying. You're a lying gossip! Get out of my office! (*Maria kicks Bobbi out.*)

EXERCISES FOR SCENE 6

A. What's Going On?

Discuss the following questions with your classmates.

1. Why does Maria say, "Will you hear me out?"
2. Why does the customer think Maria is going to hold up her refund?
3. Maria threatens to hang up if the woman keeps it up. Keeps what up?
4. What kind of relationship do Maria and Bobbi have? Explain.
5. If Bobbi feels that John and Maria's relationship is none of her business, why does she get involved by telling Maria what she saw?
6. Does Maria really feel that Bobbi is lying? Explain.

B. Search Out

Part 1

With a classmate, find and underline 16 phrasal verbs from Scene 6 that begin with the letters H, K, or L and contain the following particles: in, into, out, up, down, on, off. The verbs are listed in Exercise D, but try to find them first.

Part 2

In the spaces on the next page, list all the phrasal verbs you have underlined. Write "T" next to each transitive verb and write its object. If the phrase includes a pronoun object, write the pronoun between the two parts of the verb. If the phrase is intransitive, write "I" next to it.

1. ___ _____ _____
2. ___ _____ _____
3. ___ _____ _____
4. ___ _____ _____
5. ___ _____ _____
6. ___ _____ _____
7. ___ _____ _____
8. ___ _____ _____
9. ___ _____ _____
10. ___ _____ _____
11. ___ _____ _____
12. ___ _____ _____
13. ___ _____ _____
14. ___ _____ _____
15. ___ _____ _____
16. ___ _____ _____

C. Look Back

With a classmate, find two phrasal verbs in Scene 6 with the particles "to" and "back." Then write your own sentences using the phrasal verbs.

1. _____
   _____
2. _____
   _____

D. Match Up

Match the phrasal verb with the best definition and write the correct letter in the blank.

Part 1

1. hold down   _____
2. hold on   _____
3. knock it off   _____
4. hear out   _____

5. hold up   _____
6. keep up   _____
7. hang up   _____
8. kiss up to   _____

a. to end a phone call

b. to continue or maintain an activity at its current level

c. to delay someone or something

d. to try to please someone so they'll do something for one

e. to wait for a brief period

f. to stop an annoying behavior

g. to listen to someone until they are finished

h. to keep a job

Part 2

9. lash out   _____
10. laugh off   _____
11. have it out with   _____
12. hang out   _____
13. hold off   _____
14. keep out of   _____
15. heat up   _____
16. kick out   _____

a. to ignore or joke about something bothersome

b. to not become involved in a troublesome situation

c. to angrily confront someone

d. to become more intense

e. to verbally attack someone

f. to force to leave

g. to spend a lot of time somewhere or with someone

h. to postpone

E. Talk It Over
Discuss the following questions with your classmates.

1. Whom have you had it out with lately? Why?
2. Does your boss hear you out if you have a problem? your spouse? Explain.
3. Where do hang out at lunch? With whom do you hang out?
4. Are you able to laugh off being the butt of a joke or performing poorly? Explain.
5. What kind of situations do you try to keep out of?
6. What have you held off doing that you should do or would like to do?

F. Split Up
Fill in the blanks with the correct phrasal verbs from the list below and insert the correct pronoun between the verb and particle. Some verbs require a change in tense.

kick out   keep out of   laugh off   keep up   hear out   knock it off
hold down   hold up

1. He has worked at his job for a while, but he's not doing well. I don't think he can
   _____ much longer.
2. Helen was bringing a different man over to her parents' house every night. Finally
   they got angry and _____.
3. On the first hole, he swung at the golf ball but missed it completely. He was embarrassed, but he _____, realizing it was just a game.
4. Sarah, it really bugs Jenny when you interrupt her when she's trying to get a point
   across. She'd talk a lot more if you would _____.
5. You sing like a sick cow. Will you please _____?
6. I should have received my tax refund by now. I hope they haven't
   _____ because I claimed too many deductions.
7. Students, you all did a great job on the midterm. _____ and you
   will all get A's on the final.
8. Luis keeps calling and coming over, and I'm feeling lonely. It's going to be tough to
   _____ my life.

H. Fill In

Fill in the blanks with the correct phrasal verb from the list below. Some verbs require an object pronoun or a change in tense.

Part 1

kiss up to   hold down   hold on   knock it off   hear out   hold up   keep up

1. I understand why you don't agree with me, but if you will _____, you might change you mind.

2. Your complaining is driving me crazy. If you _____, no TV for you.

3. He has had problems _____ a job because he's more interested in partying and gambling.

4. _____ a minute. I have to check the roast I have in the oven.

5. The neighbors upstairs have been playing their stereo full blast. If they don't _____ by midnight, I'm going to call the police.

6. I have to get a car inspection or the DMV is going to _____ my registration renewal.

7. I think Johnson's going to get the promotion. He's always _____ to the boss. I wouldn't be surprised to see Johnson shining her shoes.

Part 2

lash out   kick out   have it out   laugh off   keep out of   hold off   hang out

8. Sure, she seems like an angel, but if you cross her, she can really _____.

9. They all made fun of the way I danced. I tried to be a good sport and _____, but deep down it hurt.

10. I m tired of being pushed around by my supervisor. If he's rude to me one more time, I'm going to _____ him.

11. There's nothing in this town for young people to do, so they _____ in the park and smoke.

12. The news from the doctor is bad, but let's _____ telling her until she's feeling better.

13. The students began to fight in class, so I _____.

14. This divorce has nothing to do with my mother, so _____ it.

H. Make It Up

Billy, age 22, has had trouble holding down a job. He has worked at five different places in the last 11 months. Currently, he has a good job delivering packages. However, he says he's bored and doesn't get along with his co-workers, so he's planning to quit. With a classmate, write a short dialogue in which Billy talks it over with his father, who wants him to hold on to his job. Use at least eight phrasal verbs from Scene 6. When you're finished, read the dialogue to the class.

I. Sum Up and Look Ahead

Briefly summarize what happened in Scene 6. In Scene 7, John has a conversation with his boss. Ask a classmate what they think the topic of their conversation will be.

SCENE 7: YOU LET US DOWN

Setting Up Scene 7

In Scene 7, John's boss tells John, "You let us down." What is John's boss talking about? Why do you think he says this?

Pair Up

Discuss the following questions with a classmate.

1. How do politicians let down the American people?
2. Has a friend ever let you down? How?
4. What do you do when you've been let down?
5. Have you ever let someone down? Explain.
5. What letdowns have you experienced lately?

You Let Us Down

On Friday afternoon John is called into the office of Mr. Henson, the vice president.

Henson: I hate to do this during the holidays, but I'm going to have to lay you off.

John: But why? You said last week that things were looking up. We had a 20 percent increase in sales last quarter.

Henson: We did, but your sales have decreased 30 percent. You were going strong the first half of the year, but you've really let up since August. We had high expectations for you, but you haven't lived up to them.

John: But overall, I'm still one of your top salesmen.

Henson: Not any more, you're not. (*Pause*) John, let me level with you and tell you what's really led up to my decision. You didn't have one sale this week, which is our busiest week of the year. You've been accused of leaving work in the afternoons.

John: Only once, and it was a family emergency. (*Mr. Henson looks at him skeptically*) I'm not making this up! It's true!

Henson: At first I didn't know what to make of all these rumors, but when I looked into them, I found out you've been gone three afternoons this week! The busiest week of the year!

John: But ...

Henson: Let me finish. You know, John, everyone used to look up to you for your leadership, but now they look down on you for abandoning ship. This is a profit-|sharing company. If you don't do your fair share of the work, we all lose out. We depended on you, and you let us down. I have to look out for all my employees. I can't let one bad apple spoil it for the bunch. That's why I'm laying you off. But I won't replace you yet; we might be eliminating your job. Come back in six months and we'll talk.

John: (*Angrily*) You're making me out to be some kind of cancer that has to be removed. I've done so much for this company. (*Holding back tears. Pause. Desperately*) I realize I've messed up by missing work, but please give me one more chance. I'll never live this down, but at least give me a chance to make it up to you and everyone else. And I'll make up for the time I missed by working overtime and Christmas Day. We can't live off my wife's salary, especially during the holidays.

Henson: Sorry, John. Call me in June.

EXERCISES FOR SCENE 7

A. What's Going On?

Discuss the following questions with your classmates.

1. Why might Mr. Henson hate to lay John off during the holidays? Do you think he "really" hates to lay John off?
2. What expectations didn't John live up to?
3. Who do you think accused John of leaving early? What kind of rumors do you think were being spread about John?
4. Do you think John was gone three afternoons for a family emergency? Explain.
5. What "ship" did John abandon?
6. How could one bad apple (John) spoil it for everybody?

B. Search Out

Part 1

With a classmate, find and underline 18 phrasal verbs from Scene 7 that begin with the letters L or M and contain the following particles: in, into, out, up, down, on, off. The verbs are listed in Exercise D, but try to find them first.

Part 2

In the spaces on the next page, list all the phrasal verbs you have underlined. Write "T" next to each transitive verb and write its object. If the phrase includes a pronoun object, write the pronoun between the two parts of the verb. If the phrase is intransitive, write "I" next to it.

1. ____ _____ _____

2. ____ _____ _____

3. ____ _____ _____

4. ____ _____ _____

5. ____ _____ _____

6. ____ _____ _____

7. ____ _____ _____

8. ____ _____ _____

9. ____ _____ _____

10. ____ _____ _____

11. ____ _____ _____

12. ____ _____ _____

13. ____ _____ _____

14. ____ _____ _____

15. ____ _____ _____

16. ____ _____ _____

17. ____ _____ _____

18. ____ _____ _____

C. Look Back

With a classmate, find two phrasal verbs in Scene 7 with the particles "with" and "of." Then write your own sentences using the phrasal verbs.

1. _____

_____

2. _____

_____

D. Match Up
Match the phrasal verb with the best definition and write the correct letter in the blank.
Part 1

1. lay off   _____   a. to do as well as expected

2. look up   _____   b. to invent a story or excuse, often to deceive someone

3. let up   _____   c. to try to find out the truth about a problem

4. live up to   _____   d. to move toward an important event or decison

5. lead up to   _____   e. to improve

6. make up   _____   f. to stop employing someone

7. look into   _____   g. to decrease or cease

8. look up to   _____   h. to think one is better than another

9. look down on   _____   i. to admire or respect

Part 2

10. lose out   _____   a. to repay someone

11. let down   _____   b. to overcome the shame of a misdeed or mistake

12. look out for   _____   c. to protect someone's best interests

13. make _ out   _____   d. to make a mistake or do something badly

14. mess up   _____   e. to support oneself

15. live down   _____   f. to disappoint someone

16. make up for   _____   g. to not get something one wants

17. live off   _____   h. to create an image

E. Talk It Over
Discuss the following questions with your classmates.

1. Are you trying to live up to anyone's expectations for you? whose? what expectations?
2. What led up to your decision to come to the United States?
3. Whom do you look up to? Why?
4. Whom do you look out for? Who looks out for you? How?
5. Do you feel your job is secure, or are you worried about being laid off? Explain.
6. Have you forgotten someone's birthday or anniversary? How did you make it up to them?

F. Split Up
Fill in the blanks with the correct phrasal verbs from the list below and insert the correct pronoun between the verb and particle. Some verbs require a change in tense.

live down   lay off   make up   mess up   let down

1. My teacher is accusing me of copying a short story I wrote. She doesn't believe that I _____ myself.
2. John was supposed to give the introductory part of our presentation, but he didn't show up. He really _____.
3. Lannhi, you may be able to collect unemployment if your company _____.
4. Franz, I trusted you with this task once. If you _____ again, I'm going to be really angry.
5. I almost gave up and quit, but I would have never _____.

G. Finish Up
Choose a phrasal verb from the list below and add your own words to complete the sentences.
Part 1

look up to   live off   look out for   look down on   live up to   make up   lay off

1. I promised my wife that I'd stop drinking, but I'm afraid _____.
2. In school, _____ because I wear old clothes and don't play sports very well.
3. My parents are in Korea, and I'm the only relative my 17-year-old niece has here in the United States, so _____.
4. I don't believe a word you're saying. _____.
5. Our company is talking about downsizing to reduce first-quarter losses. I'm worried _____.
6. I'm making $250 a week at my job. How can a family _____?
7. _____ who are honest and hard-working.

Part 2

let down   look up   make up for   mess up   look into   lead up to
let up   lose out

8. I married the woman my parents wanted me to and chose the career my parents wanted me to, all because _____.
9. If Renaldo doesn't complete his part of our project, _____.
10. I called the police after I heard the woman next door screaming. The police promised _____.
11. Business was slow this winter, but now that the weather is warming up, _____.
12. It wasn't your fault. I'm _____.

13. We don't have time to stop for a snack. We spent two hours playing miniature golf. Now we have to _____.

14. If you want to beat your opponent, you have to keep the pressure on. You _____

_____.

15. _____ the accident? Was there something wrong with the car?

H. Messed Up

Correct the mistake in each sentence involving the phrasal verb or its direct object.

1. I'm afraid my company is going to lay off me. I have very little seniority.
2. Johnny, if you don't help the other kids, they'll look down on.
3. I don't know why the computers aren't working, but I'll look for it right away.
4. I was working on my novel every day, but then I let up my novel and never finished.
5. What led up you to your decision to move?
6. I messed badly up when I flirted with Serge when Oscar was there.
7. When parents divorce, it's the kids who lose them out.
8. Because the computers were down for three hours, we have to work harder to make up to the lost time.
9. My parents are hoping I'm going to be a great lawyer. But I'll never live their dreams up.
10. She said she would help me before the exam, but later she refused. She really let down me.
11. He has a wild imagination. I wouldn't be surprised if he made down the whole story.
12. Now that we've found a place to live and I've found a job, we are looking up.
13. He's a great role model for young people. They admire and look him up, too.
14. The owner pays health benefits even though she doesn't have to. She really looks out.
15. My unemployment checks aren't enough. We can't live so little money.

I. Check-Up

Work with a classmate to fill in the blanks using the correct phrasal verb from the list below. Some verbs require an object pronoun or a change in tense. Then read the dialogue together.

Part 1

look up   live down   mess up   look out for   lead up to   lay off
look into   let up

Lenny, a sophomore in college, has admitted to plagiarism. He is talking with his professor.

Professor: Lenny, plagiarism is a serious offense. I (1)_____ what the school guidelines are for copying someone else's work. Do you realize you could get kicked out of school?

Lenny: Professor Rincon, I'm sorry. I (2)_____. It was stupid thing to do, and I may never (3)_____ as long as I live, but let me tell you what (4)_____ what I did. You may have noticed that my grades have fallen in the last month. The reason I've (5)_____ in my studies and fallen behind is because my life is falling apart. Just when things were (6)_____ _____ and I was able to put away some money, I got (7)_____ _____ from my job three weeks ago, which I depended on to help out my family. My mother, who has severe arthritis, barely has enough money to live on. Not only do I support my mother, but I have to (8)_____ my two younger sisters, too.

Part 2

make up for   live up to   look down on   lose out   look up to
let down   make up   make __ out

Lenny: This may sound like a big sob story to you, but it's all true. I'm not (9)_____ _____. My mother is counting on me to get a degree and make something of myself. Sometimes I don't feel like I can (10)_____ her dreams for me, but I don't want to (11)_____, either. I know it's not an excuse, but I felt stuck and ran out of time on the project, so …

Professor: (*Interrupting*) So you copied out of an encyclopedia and turned it in as your own work? Did you really think you would get away with it?

Lenny: A desperate man does desperate things. (*Pause. Pleading*) Professor, you know I've done some good work. Please give me a chance. I'll write another paper, do extra credit, anything. Just let me know how I can (12)_____ my mistake.

Professor: The other students (13)_____ you, Lenny. How do you think they would feel if they knew you had cheated?

Lenny: I'm sure they would (14)_____ me. (*Pause. Holding back tears*) I don't know how else to apologize. I feel like you're (15) _____ to be a criminal.

Professor: Lenny, you're no criminal. You're a bright student who's always the first to raise a hand to answer a question. If I had you kicked out of school, we'd all (16)_____ _____—you, me, your family, and your classmates. I think you've learned your lesson. I am going to have to fail you on this assignment, though. You knew the rules.

J. Make It Up
With a classmate, write a short dialogue in which a wife lets down her husband by forgetting his birthday. Use at least eight phrasal verbs from Scene 7. When you're finished, read the dialogue to the class.

K. Sum Up and Look Ahead
Briefly summarize what happened in Scene 7. Then ask a classmate what they think John accuses Buddy of in Scene 8.

Scene 8: I Opened Up to You

Setting Up Scene 8

In Scene 8, John says to Buddy, "I opened up to you." What do you think John opened up about? What do you think Buddy did with the information?

Pair Up

Read the scene below and discuss the following questions with your classmates.

Rita: José, I've never said anything before, but I couldn't keep my feelings inside any longer. I love you, I've always loved you, and I will always love you.

1. What risk is Rita taking by opening up to José?
2. If José likes Rita but doesn't want a serious relationship with her, how might he respond?
3. Did John take a risk by opening up to Buddy about his troubles with women? Explain.

I Opened Up To You

John returns to the office he shares with Buddy. Buddy knows that John has just talked to Mr. Henson.

Buddy: How did you make out?

John: Not too well. Henson laid me off.

Buddy: You're kidding! During the holidays? I thought he was going to promote you.

John: He said I haven't measured up lately. My sales are way down from the first half of the year.

Buddy: Did you point out the fact that you're still one of the best salesmen we've got?

John: Yeah, but it didn't matter. He also said my job would be phased out. I think it was time to move on, anyway. Maybe I'll go back to school and get a master's degree.

Buddy: (*Enthusiastically*) That's a great idea! You can only go so far in sales. (*Awkward silence. Buddy fidgets.*)

John: (*Picking up on Buddy's nervousness*) You know what really pisses me off? Someone squealed on me.

Buddy: (*Avoids eye contact*) About what?

John: You tell me!

Buddy: Tell you what? Wait a minute. You don't think ...

John: (*Tries to pin him down*) You didn't see me, but I was listening in when you told Henson. You couldn't pass up the chance to blow the whistle on me, could you? You're hoping to move up in the company!

Buddy: You've got the wrong guy. You're mixing me up with someone else.

John: I opened up to you and poured out my feelings about Elaine and Maria, and you promised to cover for me.

Buddy: Why are you picking on me? I'm your friend.

John: Because you won't own up to what you did. You're a backstabbing—! (*John grabs Buddy by the collar and pins him against the wall.*)

Buddy: I didn't mean to tell him; the words just popped out! Let me go! Help! Help! (*Security comes in, breaks up the scuffle, and begins to escort John out of the building.*)

John: (*Shouting at Buddy*) You'll pay for this!

Exercises for Scene 8

A. What's Going On?
Discuss the following questions with your classmates.

1. How does John pick up on Buddy's nervousness?
2. Why does Buddy avoid eye contact with John?
3. How could blowing the whistle on John help Buddy move up in the company?
4. How could Buddy have covered for John?
5. What's a backstabber?
6. Do you think Buddy will have to pay for blowing the whistle on John? How?
7. Did Buddy do the right thing?

B. Search Out
Part 1
With a classmate, find and underline 16 phrasal verbs from Scene 8 that begin with the letters M, O, and P and contain the following particles: in, into, out, on, off, up, down. The verbs are listed in Exercise D, but try to find them first.

Part 2
In the spaces on the next page, list all the phrasal verbs you have underlined. Write "T" next to each transitive verb and write its object. If the phrase includes a pronoun object, write the pronoun between the two parts of the verb. If the verb is intransitive, write "I" next to it.

1. ____ _____ _____
2. ____ _____ _____
3. ____ _____ _____
4. ____ _____ _____
5. ____ _____ _____
6. ____ _____ _____
7. ____ _____ _____
8. ____ _____ _____
9. ____ _____ _____
10. ____ _____ _____
11. ____ _____ _____
12. ____ _____ _____
13. ____ _____ _____
14. ____ _____ _____
15. ____ _____ _____
16. ____ _____ _____

C. Look Back

With a classmate, find two phrasal verbs in Scene 8 with the particle "for." Then write your own sentences using the phrasal verbs.

1. _____

   _____

2. _____

   _____

D. Match Up
Match the phrasal verb with the best definition and write the correct letter in the blank.

Part 1

1. make out _____
2. measure up _____
3. point out _____
4. phase out _____
5. move on _____
6. pick up on _____
7. piss off _____
8. pin down _____

a. to inform someone of something they didn't know
b. to anger
c. to leave a job or situation
d. to notice or understand something subtle
e. to make someone commit or to be clear about something
f. to be good enough or meet someone's standards
g. to succeed or not as a result of effort
h. to gradually stop using or providing something

Part 2

9. pass up _____
10. move up _____
11. mix up _____
12. open up _____
13. pour out _____
14. pick on _____
15. own up to _____
16. pop out _____

a. to mistake one person or thing for another
b. to suddenly say something one hadn't planned to
c. to admit to a wrong one has done
d. to say in a rush, usually something private one has been holding back
e. to get a better job or move to a higher level
f. to tease or mistreat someone
g. to express your feelings or thoughts
h. to not take advantage of an opportunity or offer

E. Talk It Over
Discuss the following questions with your classmates.

1. If a stranger had a piece of food on their face, would you point it out? Why or why not? How would you point it out?
2. If you ask someone to go out with you and they say maybe, what would you say to pin them down?
3. How do customs officials pick up on a smuggler's nervousness? What do they notice?
4. How do you know when it's time to move on to something else?
5. Why do some children pick on other children? What kind of kids get picked on?
6. What type of sale can't you pass up?

F. Split Up
Fill in the blanks with the correct phrasal verbs from the list below and insert the correct pronoun between the verb and particle. Some verbs require a change in tense.

piss off	point out	mix up	pin down	pass up	move up

1. I've never lived in San Francisco. I think you're _____ with someone else.
2. He refused to acknowledge or correct his error even after I had _____.
3. What really _____ is when you promise to call but don't.
4. If you really want him to commit to a specific date, you've got to _____.
5. Reggie knew he was supposed to cut down on red meat and had planned to _____ at the company picnic, but he couldn't resist a hamburger.
6. John won't be a programmer for long. The company is about to _____ to a management position.

G. Literal or Figurative?

Fill in the blank with the correct phrasal verb from the list below. Some answers require an object pronoun or a change in tense. Write "F" if the verb is used figuratively and "L" if it's used literally.

mix up   pour out   point out   pick on   pin down
move on   pop out   open up

___ 1. **Terry:** He keeps saying he'll help me, but he never does.

    Ralph: He never will unless you _____ to a specific time.

___ 2. The police chased the suspect for a mile before tackling him and _____

with a baton.

___ 3. When she threatened to leave him for not _____ to her,

he told her that he loved her but was afraid of commitment.

___ 4. It's a beautiful room that _____ a lovely garden.

___ 5. When the couple saw the dirty motel room, they decided to _____.

___ 6. You need to forget about her and _____.

___ 7. I don't have a twin brother. You must be _____ with someone else.

___ 8. **Tonia:**   What am I suppose to do with all these ingredients?

    Edmund: _____ in a large bowl.

___ 9. When the botanist_____ the man-eating plant to his students,

he got a little too close and became its lunch.

___ 10. "The bakery is down the street," she said, and _____ the door.

___ 11. When the radiator overheated, water _____ onto the ground.

___ 12. She had kept her feelings inside all day, but when she talked to her best friend

on the phone, they came _____.

___ 13. That sore will never heal if you keep _____ it.

___ 14. If you continue _____ him about his grades, he's going to cry.

___ 15. I hadn't planned to ask her to marry me; the words just _____.

___ 16. The baby began to cry when the jack-in-the box _____ and scared her.

H. Fill In

Fill in the blanks with the correct phrasal verb from the list below. Some verbs require an object pronoun or a change in tense.

make out   measure up   pick up on   own up to   piss off   phase out

Austin: How did we (1)_____ in the meeting?

Harry: Well, I arrived a little late, but I was able to (2)_____ most of what they were saying. It sounds like a machine will soon be sorting the mail. Our jobs will be (3)_____ over the next two years.

Austin: It really (4)_____ when they put machines before people.

Harry: I hate to be the one to (5)_____ the truth, but the machines can sort 60 letters a minute. You have to admit it, we just can't (6)_____ _____.

I. Messed Up

Correct the mistake in each sentence involving the phrasal verb or its direct object.

1. You haven't measured to our company's high standards.
2. You need to point at what's wrong with his idea.
3. It really pisses of when you lie to me.
4. This job is going nowhere. It's time to move out.
5. She will never tell you the truth unless you pin her.
6. This is a great opportunity to move in the company; you'd be a fool to pass it.
7. He'll open up to if you give him a chance to express himself.
8. It was difficult to pick on what the doctors were saying because of all the jargon.
9. My teacher always asks me the hardest questions. I wish he'd stop picking at.
10. You were responsible for the divorce, too, and until you own that fact, you'll never understand your ex's anger towards you.
11. I never went to Stanford. You must be mixing up with someone else.

J. Make it Up

With a classmate, write a short dialogue in which two students are angry at a third student for not showing up for their group presentation. Use at least eight phrasal verbs from Scene 8. When you're finished, read the dialogue to the class.

K. Sum Up and Look Ahead

Briefly summarize what happened in Scene 8. Then ask a classmate why, in Scene 9, Maria's not satisfied with her job and what she might do about it.

SCENE 9: SHE PUTS ME DOWN

Setting Up Scene 9

In Scene 9, Maria tells Joan that her boss puts her down. What does she mean? How might her boss put her down? What should Maria do if her boss puts her down?

Pair Up

Read the following situation and discuss the questions with a classmate.

A mother standing behind her son, who is playing the piano, says angrily, "I've spent thousands of dollars on your piano lessons, and you still play terribly!"

      1. How might this put-down affect the child?
      2. What would be a better way to tell the son he is not improving?
      3. How do teachers sometimes put their students down?
      4. How do students put other students down?
      5. Whom do comedians put down?
      6. How do bosses put down their employees?

SHE PUTS ME DOWN

It's Friday afternoon. Maria and Joan are walking to the parking lot together after work.

Maria: Work sure has been piling up lately. I never catch up. And every time I make a suggestion to Terry, she puts me down. (*Sarcastically*) "You work the telephones and I'll make the decisions," she says.

Joan: You shouldn't have to put up with that. Write a complaint against her.

Maria: And that's not all. I've been putting in ten hours a day for the last three weeks.

Joan: Who put you up to that?

Maria: No one. Terry's promised to promote me if I make sacrifices for the company. That's why I've put off looking for a new job. I keep waiting for this promotion.

Joan: It sounds to me like she's putting you on about a promotion. She's probably using you to do work that she should be doing.

Maria: I guess I'm a big sucker when it comes to jobs and relationships. Everyone's trying to put one over on me. I feel like I'm being ripped off. I wish some of your assertiveness would rub off on me. I need to be more demanding.

Joan: That's the spirit. You deserve better for yourself.

Maria: Well, I've been reading up on computer careers. Maybe I could go back to school.

Joan: How are you going to pull that off with a husband like John?

Maria: Well, the money's not exactly pouring in, but I've planned ahead and put away some savings, and John could support me. It's the least that he could do.

Joan: I'd rule out counting on his support. A career change might be just what you need, but I wouldn't rush into anything. I'd wait to see how things pan out with John.

EXERCISES FOR SCENE 9

A. What's Going On?
Discuss the following questions with your classmates.

1. Why does Maria feel like a "big sucker?"
2. What does Maria mean when she says, "I need to be more demanding"?
3. Why does Joan doubt that Maria will be able to go back to school?
4. Why would supporting Maria be "the least that [John] could do"?
5. How do you think things will pan out between Maria and John?
6. What advice would you give Maria?

B. Search Out
Part 1
With a classmate, find and underline 14 phrasal verbs from Scene 9 that begin with the letters P or R and contain one or more of the following particles: in, into, out, on, off, up, down. The verbs are listed in Exercise D, but try and find them first.

Part 2
In the spaces on the following page, list all the phrasal verbs you have underlined. Write "T" next to each transitive verb and write its object. If the phrase includes a pronoun object, write the pronoun between the two parts of the verb. If the verb is intransitive, write "I" next to it.

1. ___ _____ _____
2. ___ _____ _____
3. ___ _____ _____
4. ___ _____ _____
5. ___ _____ _____
6. ___ _____ _____
7. ___ _____ _____
8. ___ _____ _____
9. ___ _____ _____
10. ___ _____ _____
11. ___ _____ _____
12. ___ _____ _____
13. ___ _____ _____
14. ___ _____ _____

C. Look Back

With a classmate, find three phrasal verbs in Scene 9 with the particles "ahead," "over," and "away." Then write your own sentences using the phrasal verbs.

1. _____

_____

2. _____

_____

3. _____

_____

D. Match Up
Match the phrasal verb with the best definition and write the correct letter in the blank.
Part 1

1. pile up   _____   a. to delay or postpone something to a later date

2. put down   _____   b. to be untruthful

3. put up with   _____   c. to spend time or energy doing something or working

4. put in   _____   d. to increase in quantity or amount

5. put _ up to   _____   e. to insult or criticize in a mean or cruel way

6. put off   _____   f. to encourage someone to do something

7. put _ on   _____   g. to tolerate

Part 2

8. rip off   _____   a. to acquire a habit or quality of another person

9. rub off on   _____   b. to develop or happen in a particular way

10. read up on   _____   c. to succeed at a difficult task

11. pull off   _____   d. to do something suddenly without thinking enough about it

12. rule out   _____   e. to determine something is unlikely or impossible

13. rush into   _____   f. to charge more for something than it's worth

14. pan out   _____   g. to become informed about a subject

E. Talk It Over
Discuss the following questions with your classmates.

1. Has someone put you down lately? What happened?
2. What do you have to put up with at work? at school?
3. How much time do you put in every week at work? doing homework?
4. Has anyone put one over on you lately and ripped you off? What happened?
5. Do you rush into things or do you carefully consider them before acting? Give an example.
6. What do you take care of immediately, and what do you put off?

F. Split Up
Fill in the blanks with the correct phrasal verbs from the list below and insert the correct pronoun between the verb and particle. Some verbs require a change in tense.

put down	put off	put _ on	pull off	rule out	rip off

1. I don't bring up my ideas at meetings because I'm afraid the boss will laugh at me and _____.

2. You won $500,000 in the lottery?! I don't believe you. I think you're

   _____.

3. No one thought anyone would be able to solve the math problem, but Laura

   _____.

4. Although it's unlikely the soccer team will win the tournament, we can't

   _____.

5. I know I should complete my research paper, but I keep _____.

6. Don't buy your car there. They will _____.

G. Literal or Figurative?

Fill in the blank with the correct phrasal verb from the list below. Some answers require an object pronoun or a change in tense. Write "F" if the verb is used figuratively, and "L" if it's used literally.

put in	pull off	rip off	rub off on	pile up
	rush into	put down		

____1. First I got a $140 speeding ticket. Then I broke my arm falling off a ladder. Now my girlfriend wants to break up with me. My problems keep _____.

____2. The wood has been chopped and split. Please _____ by the garage.

____3. That's an expensive vase. Please _____ carefully.

____4. My father doesn't believe in me. When I tell him I want to study medicine, he _____. "You're not smart enough for that," he says.

____5. I'd be careful if I were you. Sure, he's good looking and charming, but you've only known him for a week. Don't _____ something you'll regret later.

____6. When the firemen heard the baby crying, they _____ the bedroom.

____7. That wrapping paper is beautiful. Please don't _____. I'd like to use it next Christmas.

____8. The watch looked like gold, and the guy seemed honest, but he _____. I found out it's worth $5 at most.

____9. Kim always has the right answer in class. If I hang out with her, maybe some of her intelligence will _____ me.

____10. Please wash the paint off your hands before you come inside the house. I don't want it to _____ the furniture.

____11. Johnny has Reggie pinned to the ground and he's squeezing his nose. Will you please _____?

____12. **Teresa:** After studying a grand total of ten minutes, I got an A on the final!

    Maribel: You're putting me on. How did you _____?

____13. When Ian redoes the kitchen, he's going to _____ a new stove.

____ 14. You will never learn to skate unless you _____ the time and practice.

H. Fill In

Fill in the blanks with the correct phrasal verb from the list below. Some verbs require an object pronoun or a change in tense.

put off   put up with   put _ up to   read up on   rule out   put _ on   put in

Kimo: Why don't we go have a beer? We've (1)_____ a long day.

Terry: No, I have to get up early tomorrow to (2)_____ a Supreme Court decision for next month's trial.

Kimo: On a Saturday morning? Who (3)_____ that? Do it next week. Let's have some fun.

Terry: Never (4)_____ until tomorrow what you can do today. Besides, Johnson says she hasn't (5)_____ the possibility of having me try the case.

Kimo: You're (6)_____. Johnson said that!?

Terry: Yeah.

Kimo: You're so gullible! No junior partner has ever tried a case before the State Supreme Court. Johnson's really put one over on you. Don't (7)_____ that kind of treatment.

I. Make It Up

With a classmate, write a short dialogue in which Rhonda asks Hamid for advice about how to deal with a teacher who puts her down. Use at least eight phrasal verbs from Scene 9. When you're finished, read the dialogue to the class.

J. Sum Up and Look Ahead

Briefly summarize what happened in Scene 9. Then ask a classmate what they think Maria will find in Scene 10 when she goes home to pick up some clothes.

Scene 10: I've Run Out of Patience

Setting Up Scene 10

In Scene 10, Maria tells Joan she has run out of patience. With whom or what do you think Maria has run out of patience? Why? What might she do when her patience is used up?

Pair Up

Discuss the following questions with a classmate.

1. Why do people in long lines sometimes run out of patience?
2. Can a person avoid running out of patience? How?
3. In what situations do you run out of patience?
4. What can a person do to keep from running out of patience?
5. What do you do when you have run out of patience?

I'VE RUN OUT OF PATIENCE

It's Friday afternoon, and Maria and Joan are driving home from work. Joan has invited Maria to stay with her.

Maria: I feel like I'm running away from my problems by moving in with you, but I've run out of patience with John. Every couple runs up against serious problems, but another affair is just too much. Then again, maybe I'm reading more into the situation than there really is. Maybe if I ride out the storm, there'll be a rainbow waiting at the end for me.

Joan: More likely you'll be buried under an avalanche. John's never going to straighten up.

Maria: You're right. I need to put my foot down this time. (*Pause.*) You must be tired of me running to you every time I have a problem. I'll just stay with you this week-end and see what happens. Is that okay?

Joan: Stay as long as you need to.

Maria: Thanks. (*Pause.*) I need to stop off at my house to pick up some clothes and stuff before going to your house. It'll only take 15 minutes.

Joan: No problem. (*They arrive and Maria begins to sort through the laundry. A bill falls out of John's pants.*)

Maria: Oh, my gosh! John ran up a $1,000 bill at Applegate Mall!

Joan: For what?

Maria: Two tickets to Hawaii and a gold bracelet. Maybe he's going to reach out to me and surprise me with a romantic getaway!

Joan: When did he buy them? (*Before Maria can answer, the phone rings.*)

Maria: (*Running to the phone*) Maybe that's him now! Hello?

Bobbi: Maria?

Maria: Yes?

Bobbi: This is Bobbi. Guess who I ran into at the airport!?

Maria: (*Frightened*) Who?

Bobbi: John and his cute redhead. We're all on the same flight to Hawaii. I can't believe he's going to run out on you and run off with her!

EXERCISES FOR SCENE 10

A. What's Going On?

Discuss the following questions with your classmates.

1. How might Maria be running away from her problems if she moves in with Joan?
2. What storm is Maria talking about? How could she ride it out?
3. What avalanche does Joan think Maria will be buried under?
4. If Maria puts her foot down this time, what will she do?
5. What reason does Bobbi have for informing Maria about John? What does Bobbi's tone of voice sound like?
6. What would you do if you were Maria?

B. Search Out

Part 1

With a classmate, find and underline 11 phrasal verbs from Scene 10 that begin with the letters R or S and contain one or more of the following particles: in, into, out, up, down, on, off. The verbs are listed in Exercise D, but try to find them first.

Part 2

In the spaces on the next page, list all the phrasal verbs you have underlined. Write "T" next to each transitive verb and write its object. If the phrase includes a pronoun object, write the pronoun between the two parts of the verb. Note that the pronoun follows three-part verbs. If the verb is intransitive, write "I" next to it.

1. ___ _____ _____
2. ___ _____ _____
3. ___ _____ _____
4. ___ _____ _____
5. ___ _____ _____
6. ___ _____ _____
7. ___ _____ _____
8. ___ _____ _____
9. ___ _____ _____
10. ___ _____ _____
11. ___ _____ _____

C. Look Back

With a classmate, find two phrasal verbs in Scene 10 with the particles "away" and "to." Then write your own sentences using the phrasal verbs.

1. _____

2. _____

D. Match Up

Match the phrasal verb with the best definition and write the correct letter in the blank.

1. run out of   _____   a. to make a brief visit

2. run up against   _____   b. to meet someone unexpectedly

3. read into   _____   c. to encounter difficult or unexpected problems

4. ride out   _____   d. to correct improper behavior

5. straighten up   _____   e. to go away with someone to have an affair

6. stop off   _____   f. to use up

7. run up   _____   g. to believe a situation has more importance than it
                                        does

8. reach out   _____   h. to attempt to get closer to someone or to resolve bad
                                        feelings

9. run into   _____   i. to abandon someone

10. run out on   _____   j. to persevere until a difficult situation has ended

11. run off with   _____   k. to accumulate a big debt or to spend a lot of money

E. Talk It Over

Discuss the following questions with your classmates.

1. What problems have you run up against lately? How do plan to resolve them?
2. How do you get a child who's behaving badly to straighten up?
3. Have you run up a huge bill lately? Explain.
4. Whom have you run into lately that you hadn't seen for many years? Where did you run into them?
5. What do you often run out of? Why?

F. Literal or Figurative?

Fill in the blank with the correct phrasal verb from the list below. Some answers require an object pronoun or a change in tense. Write "F" if the verb is used figuratively and "L" if it's used literally.

straighten up   reach out   run out of   run up   run into   run off with

___ 1. Will you stop off at the grocery on your way home? We've _____ milk and eggs.

___ 2. As soon as the robber had the money, he _____ the bank.

___ 3. It was so embarrassing. I wasn't looking where I was going and _____ someone and almost knocked her over.

___ 4. I _____ an old friend I went to college with. I hadn't seen him in five years.

___ 5. I gave him all the love I could give, but he still _____ his secretary.

___ 6. While we were in Macy's, the alarm went off and the police chased someone who was trying to _____ some clothing.

___ 7. Something is bothering your sister. You should _____ to her and find out what's wrong.

___ 8. The baby took a few steps and then _____ to her mother so she wouldn't fall.

___ 9. Johnny, _____. You have terrible posture.

___10. If your son is behaving badly and smoking marijuana, send him to a military school. They'll _____.

___11. In the last part of the marathon, they have to _____ a hill.

___12. She took all of her friends and family out to dinner and _____ a huge bill.

G. Fill In

Fill in the blank with the correct phrasal verbs from the list below. Some answers require an object pronoun and a change in tense.

　　　　run out on　　　read into　　　ride out　　　stop off　　　run up against

1. If you (1)_____ her, she may go out with your best friend.
2. On your way home, (2)_____ and pick up the dry cleaning.
3. There's nothing we can do. We've lost all power in this blizzard. We just have to be patient and (3)_____.
4. I've never (4)_____ a problem that I can't solve.
5. **Melody:** Leon used to bring me flowers every Friday night, but now I only get them once in a while. Maybe he doesn't love me anymore.

    Diana: Don't be silly. You're (5)_____ it more than there really is.

H. Messed Up

Correct the mistake involving the phrasal verb or its direct object in each sentence.

1. If you keep treating her badly, she's going to run out to you.
2. Mary fell in love with the mailman and ran with him to Mexico.
3. I ran against my old philosophy professor yesterday. I took her class four years ago.
4. I understand you're angry at your daughter for getting in trouble, but she's sorry and needs you to reach for her.
5. John got promoted and took everyone out to dinner. He ran out a huge bill.
6. He's only 19 and he's already been in prison twice for armed robbery. I don't think he'll ever straighten.
7. Time heals everything if you can ride with the storm.
8. Brazil didn't expect to run up such a tough opponent like France.
9. Just because the professor hasn't called on you in class lately doesn't mean he dislikes you. I think you're reading too much.
10. I have to be in class in 20 minutes and I've only completed half of my homework. I think I'm going to run into time.

I. Make It Up

With a classmate, write a short dialogue in which Gretel gives advice to Igor, who is worried that his spouse is going to run out on him. Use at least seven phrasal verbs from Scene 10. When you're finished, read the dialogue to the class.

J. Sum Up and Look Ahead

Briefly summarize what happened in Scene 10. Then ask a classmate to predict how Maria will react now that John has gone to the airport to run off to Hawaii with Elaine.

Scene 11: Stick Up for Yourself

Setting Up Scene 11
In Scene 11 Joan says to Maria, "You need to snap out of it and stick up for yourself." What does Joan mean?

Pair Up
In the Pair Up exercise for Scene 9, a mother puts her son down by telling him he still played terribly after thousands of dollars of piano lessons. How could the son have stood up for himself? How can the following people who have been put down stand up for themselves?

1. **Boss to an older employee:** You should be thinking about retirement instead of a promotion.
   Employee: _____

2. **Teacher to a student:** Your spelling is horrible. Nobody will want to read anything you write with spelling like this.
   Student: _____

3. **Father to his son:** "You'll never be as successful as your sister."
   Son: _____

STICK UP FOR YOURSELF

Maria is shocked to hear that John is at the airport with Elaine.

Maria: (*She can barely speak*) Are you sure it's John?

Bobbi: Tall, black hair, glasses right? (*Bobbi decides to rub it in.*) You should see them making out like teenagers. I don't see what he sees in her. You're much prettier. But you know men. Hey, our flight's been delayed an hour. We're not scheduled to leave until 7:45. Why don't come down to the airport and see us off?

Bobbi's call has completely shaken Maria up. She drops the phone and collapses on the kitchen floor.

Joan: Maria! Are you okay!?

Maria: I hate him! I hate him! I could kill him!

Joan: Settle down, Maria. It's going to be OK.

Maria: It's not going to be OK! Never again! Why is this nightmare happening to me? I just wanted to settle down with a nice man. Where did I go wrong?

Joan: I'll spell it out for you as simply as I can. You should have told that jerk to shape up or ship out a long time ago when he started to shop around at the bars again. (*Pause.*) But you can't just sit around feeling sorry for yourself. Snap out of it and stick up for yourself. See to it that he doesn't get away with it.

Maria: His plane's been delayed an hour.

Joan: Wouldn't he be surprised if we showed up!

A sinister smile replaces Maria's frown as though she has stumbled on a great idea. She dries her eyes and takes a deep breath.

Maria: (*In a calm, confident voice*) I need to change. I'll be ready to go in ten minutes. (*In her bedroom, Maria finds the keys to John's gun cabinet. She settles on a tiny pistol and stuffs the gun into her purse.*) It's time to show off just how well I can shoot.

Exercises for Scene 11

A. What's Going On?
Discuss the following questions with your classmates.

1. If John and Elaine are making out like teenagers, what are they doing?
2. Bobbi says she doesn't know what John sees in Elaine. What do you think John sees in her?
3. What does Bobbi mean when she says, "But you know men"?
4. What does Joan mean when she says, "You should have told that jerk to shape up or ship out a long time ago"?
5. What was John shopping around for, according to Joan?
6. When "a sinister smile replaces Maria's frown," what great idea do you think she has stumbled on?
7. What is Maria going to do with the pistol?

B. Search Out
Part 1
With a classmate, find and underline 15 phrasal verbs from Scene 11 that begin with the letters R or S and contain one or more of the following particles: in, into, out, up, down, on, off. The verbs are listed in Exercise D, but try to find them first.

Part 2
In the spaces on the next page, list all the phrasal verbs you have underlined. Write "T" next to each transitive verb and write its object. If the phrase includes a pronoun object, write the pronoun between the two parts of the verb. If the verb is intransitive, write "I" next to it.

1. ____ _____ _____
2. ____ _____ _____
3. ____ _____ _____
4. ____ _____ _____
5. ____ _____ _____
6. ____ _____ _____
7. ____ _____ _____
8. ____ _____ _____
9. ____ _____ _____
10. ____ _____ _____
11. ____ _____ _____
12. ____ _____ _____
13. ____ _____ _____
14. ____ _____ _____
15. ____ _____ _____

C. Look Back

With a classmate, find three phrasal verbs from Scene 11 with the particles around, away, and to.
Then write your own sentences using the phrasal verbs.

1. _____
   _____
2. _____
   _____
3. _____
   _____

D. Match Up

Match the phrasal verb with the best definition and write the correct letter in the blank.

Part 1

1. rub in   _____
2. see in   _____
3. see off   _____
4. shake up   _____
5. settle down   _____
6. settle down with   _____
7. spell out   _____

a. to calm down
b. to establish a home of one's own
c. to upset or frighten
d. to explain something clearly
e. to go with someone to a bus, train, or plane terminal to say goodbye
f. to remind someone of something embarassing to intentionally hurt them
g. to recognize positive qualities in someone

Part 2

8. shape up   _____
9. ship out   _____
10. snap out of   _____
11. stick up for _____
12. show up   _____
13. stumble on   _____
14. settle on   _____
15. show off   _____

a. to improve performance
b. to finally decide on something
c. to arrive
d. to stop feeling a certain way
e. to leave
f. to discover someone or something unexpectedly
g. to try to impress people with something or someone
h. to defend

E. Talk It Over
Discuss the following questions with your classmates.

1. Have you stuck up for yourself or someone else lately? Explain.
2. Do you sometimes just show up at a friend's house, or do you always call first? Explain.
3. What is a good way for a teacher to settle a class down?
4. How can you help a friend snap out of feeling sorry for themselves?
5. Why do children need things spelled out to them?
6. Why do people show off?

F. Split Up
Fill in the blanks with the correct phrasal verbs from the list below and insert the correct pronoun between the verb and particle. Some answers require a change in tense.

shape up   see off   show off   shake up   spell out   settle down

1. Our son is going to be leaving for six months. I don't think it's right to just drop him off and leave. Let's park the car and _____.

2. Maybe we shouldn't tell the Browns that we saw their son smoking. I think the news would really _____.

3. When the mental patient began to scream and hit her attendants, they gave her a shot to _____.

4. My neighbors bought a new luxury sedan, and they've been driving it around the neighborhood to _____.

5. Raymond, I've given you five reasons why you're not going to pass this class. I don't know how else I can _____ to you.

6. If your kids are misbehaving, cut off their allowance. That will _____.

G. Literal or Figurative?

Fill in the blank with the correct phrasal verb from the list below. Some answers require an object pronoun or a change in tense. Write "F" if the verb is used figuratively and "L" if it's used literally.

spell out   rub in   see in   stumble on   shake up

____ 1. He sprained his ankle when he _____ a something in the sidewalk.

____ 2. We were just driving along, not knowing where we were going to stay, when we _____ a cute little inn near the ocean.

____ 3. The death of her father really _____.

____ 4. Will you please _____ the salad dressing before you pour it?

____ 5. *Enthusiasm*? I know it starts E, N, T, H. Can you please _____?

____ 6. You're confused about what will happen if you keep on missing deadlines? Let me _____ for you as clearly as I can. If you do it again, you're fired.

____ 7. After you apply the stain remover to the shirt, you have to _____.

____ 8. It was bad enough that he failed the test. You shouldn't have _____ by laughing at him.

____ 9. These tinted windows are great. You can see out, but people can't _____.

____ 10. Mary, he's boring, he's dumb, and he's never said anything funny in his life. I really don't understand what you _____.

H. Finish Up
Write a logical follow-up sentence using the phrasal verb in parentheses.

1. John embarrasses me at parties by telling dirty jokes. (show off)

_____

2. Our parents are going on a cruise to Alaska. (see off)

_____

3. Those bullies at school keep picking on Joey. (stick up for)

_____

4. I know you feel bad that you lost the game, but you did your best. (snap out of)

_____

5. We'd love to come to your party. (show up)

_____

6. I won't have a lazy, unemployed husband living off me. (shape up)

_____

7. These kids are out of control. (settle down with)

_____

8. I'm tired of dating. (settle down)

_____

I. Messed Up
Correct the mistake involving the phrasal verb or its direct object in each sentence.

1. I was depressed for a week, but I finally snapped out.
2. I'm going down to the train station with my husband to see off him.
3. If he still doesn't understand our proposal, you need to spell it for him step by step.
4. If he won't clean up his act, tell him to shape out or ship off.
5. I was looking through some old photo albums and stumbled an old photo of our wedding day.
6. Tell your mother to knock it off if she lashes out at you. You need to stick her up yourself and be strong.
7. You're almost 40 years old. It's time to settle up and get married.
8. Have you settled for the name you're going to give your baby?

J. Make It Up
With a classmate, write a short dialogue in which Marta begins to rub it in because she got a promotion over Svetlana, and Svetlana sticks up for herself. Use at least seven phrasal verbs from Scene 11. When you're finished, read the dialogue to the class.

K. Sum Up and Look Ahead
Briefly summarize what happened Scene 11. Then ask a classmate to predict what John and Elaine will talk about during their flight delay.

Scene 12: I Need to Sort a Few Things Out

Setting Up Scene 12

In Scene 12, John and Elaine are at the airport, but John wants to be alone for a few minutes. He tells Elaine he wants to sort a few things out. What does he mean? What is he going to do?

Pair Up

Discuss the following questions with a classmate.

1. What kinds of things have you sorted recently?
2. When was the last time you stopped to sort out your thoughts and feelings? What was on your mind? Did you get things sorted out?
3. Where do you go when you need to sort things out?

I Need to Sort a Few Things Out

After he was laid off, John decided to throw caution to the wind. He started off by calling Elaine and telling her he was taking her to Hawaii. He then realized that to scrape up enough money for the trip he would need $2,300, half of his and Maria's entire savings. He got to the bank just before it closed. He took the cash to the mall and bought two tickets to Hawaii at a travel agency and a gold bracelet at a jewelry store. Finally, he rushed home to shower, change his clothes, and pack before heading to the airport. Now, at the airport, the flight delay has given John time to think over his decision. What he's about to do to his relationship with Maria really begins to sink in. He can't shake off the realization that he may be throwing his life away.

John: (*To Elaine*) Honey, I need a drink. I'll be back in 20 minutes.

Elaine: I'll go with you.

John: No, I want to be by myself for a while. I need to sort a few things out.

Elaine: Are you having second thoughts about our trip? Speak up now if you are.

John: (*Becoming angry*) Please don't set me off, Elaine. Not now.

Elaine: (*Hurt and angry*) Maybe you're getting cold feet. Maybe you don't really love me.

John: Hold on. Slow down. What's love got to do with this? I barely know you. This a fling, not a honeymoon. (*John begins to storm off but turns around.*) I'm sorry I shot my mouth off like that. I just need some time alone. (*He heads off to the bar.*)

Exercises for Scene 12

A. What's Going On?
Discuss the following questions with your classmates.

1. What does John realize he's about to do to his relationship with Maria?
2. Why does John throw caution to the wind?
3. What second thoughts might John be having about taking Elaine to Hawaii?
4. If John were getting "cold feet," what would he be thinking and feeling?
5. How did John shoot off his mouth?
6. Describe how John was walking when he began to storm off to the bar.

B. Search Out
Part 1
With a classmate, find and underline ten phrasal verbs from Scene 12 that begin with the letter S and contain one or more of the following particles: in, into, out, on, off, up, down. The verbs are listed in Exercise D, but try to find them first.

Part 2
In the spaces on the following page, list all the phrasal verbs you have underlined. Write "T" next to each transitive verb and write its object. If the phrase includes a pronoun object, write the pronoun between the two parts of the verb. If the phrase is intransitive, write "I" next to it.

1. ___ _____ _____
2. ___ _____ _____
3. ___ _____ _____
4. ___ _____ _____
5. ___ _____ _____
6. ___ _____ _____
7. ___ _____ _____
8. ___ _____ _____
9. ___ _____ _____
10. ___ _____ _____

C. Look back

With a classmate, find two phrasal verbs from Scene 12 with the particles "over" and "away." Then write your own sentences using the phrasal verbs.

1. _____

_____

2. _____

_____

D. Match Up
Match the phrasal verb with the best definition and write the correct letter in the blank.

1. sink in _____
2. shake off _____
3. start off _____
4. scrape up _____
5. sort out _____
6. speak up _____
7. set off _____
8. slow down _____
9. storm off _____
10. shoot off _ mouth _____

a. to get rid a problem or illness
b. to annoy
c. to voice your opinion instead of remaining silent
d. to find something scarce, often by being resourceful
e. to quickly and angrily leave a place or situation
f. to truly understand some information or facts
g. to begin
h. to say something you shouldn't
i. to organize tasks or things that are mixed up
j. to decrease the rate or speed of something

E. Split Up
Fill in the blanks with the correct phrasal verbs from the list below and insert the correct pronoun between the verb and particle. Some verbs require a change in tense.

scrape up   start off   shake off   sort out   slow down   set off

1. I've had this cold for almost a month now. I can't seem to _____.

2. When Sandra checks out other men when she's with Charlie, it really

   _____.

3. The professor's speech was terrific. She _____ by telling
   about the time she walked into class backwards to get her students' attention.

4. He used to make ten beautiful sculptures a year, but his age and arthritis have

   _____. He's lucky to make two or three now.

5. $1,200 by Friday? That's a lot of money. I don't know if I can _____
   in just two days.

6. Every couple has problems. You two need to work together to _____.

F. Literal or Figurative?

Fill in the blank with the correct phrasal verb from the list below. Some answers require an object pronoun or a change in tense. Write "F" if the verb is used figuratively and "L" if it's used literally.

scrape up   shoot off   set off   sort out   sink in   shake off   start off

____ 1. You're covered with snow. Go outside and _____.

____ 2. This loss hurts, but we have to _____ and prepare for tomorrow's game.

____ 3. Harry attempted to drive his car out of the mud, but his back wheels spun and _____ even deeper.

____ 4. This divorce has been rough. This morning I began to cry when it finally _____ that I'll only be a part-time father to my children now.

____ 5. I shouldn't yell, but when he refuses to do his chores, it _____.

____ 6. Our dog ran away because the neighborhood boys were _____ firecrackers.

____ 7. Why does Harry always have to _____ his mouth _____ about welfare mothers? He should get a job before he dumps on the poor.

____ 8. Don't play with guns, or you might _____ one of your toes.

____ 9. I'm confused. Harry says he wants to marry me, but I've only known him for two weeks. I need some time to myself to _____ all of this _____.

____ 10. When I _____ my clothes ____ for the trip, I realized I didn't have a sweater.

____ 11. I was really nervous, but I _____ the courage to ask Pat to marry me.

____ 12. Use a spoon to _____ any pieces of food that stick to the bottom of the saucepan.

____ 13. On our tour of Europe, we're going to _____ in Paris, then take a train into the Swiss Alps, and finally end up in Germany.

____ 14. If you're going to teach your daughter to ride a bicycle, you need to _____ her _____ on a bike with training wheels.

G. Talk It Over
Discuss the following questions with your classmates.

1. What should a teacher do if students keep shooting off their mouths in class?
2. What advice would you give to someone who can't shake off a cold?
3. If you didn't have enough money to pay your rent, how would you scrape it up?
4. Do you speak up if you don't agree with someone's opinion? Explain.
5. Who or what sets you off? Why?

H. Finish Up
Write a logical follow-up sentence using the phrasal verb in parentheses.

1. Ling burst out crying when her parents said she was too young to date. (storm off)

_____

2. I'd like to go to the movies with you, but I'm broke. (scrape up)

_____

3. This morning I ate breakfast and did my chores as though Harry were still here.
(sink in) _____

4. You shouldn't have paid $26 for a cold piece of meat and raw vegetables.
(speak up)_____

I. Make It Up
With a classmate, write a short dialogue in which Annie is trying to sort out her feelings with a friend after being dumped by her boyfriend. Use six phrasal verbs from Scene 12. When you're finished, read the dialogue to the class.

J. Sum Up and Look Ahead
Briefly summarize what happened in Scene 12. Then ask a classmate what they think John will talk about with the airport bartender in Scene 13.

Scene 13: I Straightened Myself Out

Setting Up Scene 13

In Scene 13, John is having a drink and says to the bartender, "Years ago I straightened myself out and turned my life around." What does he mean? Do you think he can do it again? How?

Pair Up

Discuss the following questions with a classmate.

1. How might spending time in prison straighten someone out?
2. Have most criminals straightened themselves out by the time they are released from prison? Why or why not? How do they straighten themselves out, or how does prison straighten them out?
3. What temptations do people have who have straightened themselves out?
4. How do you straighten out a 15-year-old who's been caught stealing?
5. How does a teacher straighten out a student who rarely attends class or does his homework?

I STRAIGHTENED MYSELF OUT

John: (*To the bartender*) A double shot of whiskey, please. (*Swallows the shot down in one gulp and orders another.*) I swore off this stuff two years ago when I got drunk and had an affair. Then I straightened myself out and turned my life around for a while. Now I'm about to screw up again and skip off to Hawaii with a woman I hardly know that I've hooked up with.

Bartender: It's none of my business, but it sounds like you're setting yourself up for some real trouble.

John: (*Sighs dejectedly*) Trouble's my middle name. (*Talking to himself*) Women take up so much time and energy. I ruin my marriage so I can take this woman to Hawaii, and she's asking me to love her! What a great way to turn someone off. (*Pause*) I should never have taken her out the night we met. (*Shouting in a loud, drunken voice*) I think I'll take you up on your offer of a third whiskey, bartender.

Bartender: (*Annoyed*) I didn't offer you anything, mister. And I think you've had enough.

John: (*Beginning to space out and mumble to himself*) Maria and I are going to split up anyway. Might as well have some fun.

Bartender: Mister, you'd better drink this coffee and sober up before you get on a plane.

John: (*Drunk and angry*) If I wanted your advice, I'd ask for it. You should stay out of other people's affairs.

Bartender: Hey buddy, don't take your problems out on me.

John almost falls as he staggers into an airport bathroom, feeling like he's going to throw up. He sizes himself up in the mirror and doesn't like what he sees.

John: (*To his reflection in the mirror*) Do the right thing for once in your life and go home to Maria.

EXERCISES FOR SCENE 13

A. What's Going On?
Discuss the following questions with your classmates.

1. How might John have turned his life around for a while?
2. What trouble is John setting himself up for?
3. What does John mean when he says, "Trouble's my middle name"?
4. How do we know John is drunk?
5. Why does John become angry when the bartender tells him he should sober up?
   Why does the bartender tell him to sober up?
6. What does John see in the mirror when he sizes himself up?

B. Search Out
Part 1
With a classmate, find and underline 16 phrasal verbs from Scene 13 that begin with the letters S or T and contain one or more of the following particles: in, into, out, on, off, up, down. The verbs are listed in Exercise D, but try to find them first.

Part 2
In the spaces on the next page, list all the phrasal verbs you have underlined. Write "T" next to each transitive verb and write its object. If the phrase includes a pronoun object, write the pronoun between the two parts of the verb. If the phrase is intransitive, write "I" next to it.

1. ___ _____ _____

2. ___ _____ _____

3. ___ _____ _____

4. ___ _____ _____

5. ___ _____ _____

6. ___ _____ _____

7. ___ _____ _____

8. ___ _____ _____

9. ___ _____ _____

10. ___ _____ _____

11. ___ _____ _____

12. ___ _____ _____

13. ___ _____ _____

14. ___ _____ _____

15. ___ _____ _____

16. ___ _____ _____

C. Look Back

With a classmate, find two phrasal verbs in Scene 13 with the particles "around" and "with." Then write your own sentences using the phrasal verbs.

1. _____

   _____

2. _____

   _____

D. Match Up

Match the phrasal verb with the best definition and write the correct letter in the blank.

Part 1

1. swear off _____
2. straighten out _____
3. screw up _____
4. skip off _____
5. set up _____
6. take up _____
7. turn off _____
8. take out _____

a. to promise to stop a certain behavior, usually a negative one
b. to mess up or make a mistake
c. to lose interest in something or someone
d. to take someone on a date or pay for an outing
e. to leave suddenly and secretly
f. to fill one's time or space
g. to correct bad behavior or personal problems
h. to arrange or cause something negative to happen

Part 2

9. take up on _____
10. space out _____
11. split up _____
12. sober up _____
13. stay out of _____
14. take out on _____
15. throw up _____
16. size up _____

a. to lose awareness of one's surroundings and stare off into space
b. to not get involved
c. to make a judgment about a person or situation
d. to end a relationship or marriage
e. to direct anger or frustration with one person or situation against another
f. to gradually become less drunk
g. to accept someone's offer
h. to bring up food or drink from your stomach

E. Talk It Over
Discuss the following questions with your classmates.

1. Do you ever space out in class or at work? Why?
2. What takes up most of your time every day?
3. What kind of commercials or advertisements turn you off? Why?
4. Where would you like to be taken out to? Why?

F. Split Up
Fill in the blanks with the correct phrasal verbs from the list below and insert the correct pronoun between the verb and particle. Some verbs require a change in tense.

screw up	size up	set up	take out
turn off	sober up	split up	straighten out

1. It's our parents' fiftieth wedding anniversary, so we're going to _____ to a nice restaurant.

2. If you've had too much to drink, it's not true that black coffee and a cold shower will _____. Only time will do the job.

3. The drug dealer thought he was making a sale to a junkie, but the police had _____. He was arrested as soon as he pulled out the cocaine.

4. The test wasn't that hard, but I _____ by not following directions.

5. A lot of people liked the movie *Pulp Fiction*, but all the graphic violence _____.

6. Those two girls in the back are always talking. I'm going to have to _____.

7. After Professor Woo took François under her wing, she was able to really _____ _____.

8. Jake and his friends are big guys, so after _____, the bully and his gang backed down from the argument.

G. Check-Up

Work with a classmate to fill in the blanks with the correct phrasal verbs from the list below. Some verbs require an object pronoun or a change in tense. Then read the dialogue together.

Part 1

take up   swear off   take out   sober up   take up on

straighten out   throw up

Mark: (*Sadly*) Nettie, I'm calling about Bob.

Nettie: (*Worried*) He got drunk, didn't he?!

Mark: Yep. I found him passed out. He had (1)_____ all over himself. What a mess.

Nettie: I thought he (2)_____ alcohol last month and said he'd never touch another drop?

Mark: He did, but you know that crowd he hangs out with at work. They wanted to (3)_____ for his birthday to a bar.

Nettie: (*Sarcastic*) And he (4)_____ it. Bob has no willpower. I used to believe him when he'd promise to (5)_____ his life, but he's let us down so many times. (*Pause*) How is Eleanor taking all of this?

Mark: She says she feels like her whole life has been (6)_____ with trying to (7)_____, and she's not willing to do it anymore. She wants to leave him and take care of herself for a change.

Part 2

stay out of   space out   split up   take out on   set up   skip off   size up

Nettie: Good for her. I wish she had decided to do that 20 years ago. If she had (8)_____ _____ then, she would have realized that living with a drunk was a lost cause. (*Pause.*) Do you think they'll finally (9)_____?

Mark: Maybe so this time. It's the same old story. He gets drunk, comes home, and (10)_____ all of his problems _____ Eleanor. She might just (11)_____ on her own this time.

Nettie: His friends should have known better than to take him to a bar.

Mark: Yeah, but he's an adult. He (12)_____ by agreeing to go. He should have said no or asked if they could go somewhere else.

Nettie: Have you talked to him?

Mark: Yeah, but he was (13)_____ and his speech was slurred.

Nettie: Well, let me know if there's anything I can do.

Mark: Thanks, Sis. I know he's our brother, but I'm giving up trying to help him. I'm going to (14)_____ his life from now on.

H. Literal or Figurative?

Fill in the blanks in the sentences with the correct phrasal verbs from the list below. Some answers require an object pronoun or a change in tense. Then write "F" if the phrasal verb is used figuratively and "L" if it's used literally.

set up   turn off   take out   split up   straighten out   skip off

____ 1. My two-year-old likes to _____ his toy trains and then knock them down.

____ 2. You're _____ for a lifetime of misery if you marry just for money.

____ 3. There's not enough candy for everyone, so we have to _____.

____ 4. I think parents should stay together for their kids. When they _____ _____, the kids really suffer.

____ 5. If he's causing trouble in class, you need to send him to the principal's office. She'll tell him that if he doesn't _____, she'll kick him out of school.

____ 6. The curtains are crooked. The left side is hanging down too much. Will you please _____?

____ 7. When the little girl found out she was going to Disneyland, she _____ _____ down the sidewalk to tell her friends.

____ 8. I think she's the kind of woman who would dump you and _____ with the first man who smiles at her.

____ 9. Men who unbutton their shirts down to their navel to show off their hairy chests really _____.

____ 10. There's a small lake in the bathroom. Joey, did you forget to _____ the water?

____ 11. Ralph, the garbage is full. Will you please _____?

____ 12. Now that we're married, Pedro and I never go out. When we were still dating, he used to _____ at least once a week.

I. Finish Up

Write a logical follow-up sentence using the phrasal verb in parentheses. Some verbs may require a change in tense.

1. The cake looks delicious and I'd love to have piece, but (swear off) _____

_____

2. When my parents argue, (stay out of) _____

_____

3. If you cheat on your tests, (set up) _____

_____

4. I like taking night classes, but (take up) _____

_____

5. Terry's not happy at work, so when she comes home tired and angry, (take out on)

_____

6. You're going to get fired (straighten out) _____

_____

7. If my parents offered to pay my way through school, (take up on) _____

_____

J. Make It Up

With a classmate, write a short dialogue in which Mercedes tries to straighten out her friend Alma, who often loses all of her money gambling. Use at least eight phrasal verbs from Scene 13. When you're finished, read the dialogue to the class.

K. Sum Up and Look Ahead

Briefly summarize what happened in Scene 13. Then ask a classmate to predict what Maria and Joan will do when they arrive at the airport.

Scene 14: I'm Going to Stand Out

Setting Up Scene 14

In Scene 14, as Maria is walking to the airport entrance, she says to herself, "I'm going to stand out like a sore thumb." What is she talking about?

Pair Up

Discuss the following questions with a classmate.

1. Some people like to stand out in a crowd, while others prefer to blend in. Which of the following people really wants the attention? Explain.

   a woman wearing a formal dress at a party in which everyone is dressed in jeans and T-shirts?

   a young man with spiked, purple hair?

   a seven-foot-tall man getting on an elevator?

   Maria at the airport?

2. Why do the following people stand out?

   Michael Jordan?

   Bill Gates?

   Mother Teresa?

   Shakespeare?

I'm Going To Stand Out

Joan and Maria are at Maria's house.

Joan: (*Calling to Maria*) We'd better take off before they do!

Maria: I'm coming!

They get in the car and head towards the airport. Fifteen minutes later, they arrive at the airport parking lot.

Joan: Have you thought up what you're going to say to John when you tell him off?

Maria: There isn't a lot to say. Actions speak louder than words. (*Pause*) Listen Joan, I appreciate your support. You've taken on all of my problems as if they were your own, but I don't want you to get involved any further. I don't know how this is going to turn out. It could get pretty ugly. Please go home. I'll take a taxi home.

Joan: I can't leave you now! I don't want you to have to sweat this out alone. I promise not to step in unless they team up against you.

Maria: No, John will think I've brought you along just to stir up trouble. You've given me the strength to stand alone. Don't attempt to talk me out of seeing this thing through by myself. Please go home now, Joan.

Joan: No way! I'm going to stay here and wait for you.

Maria gets out of the car and starts to run toward the entrance. Suddenly she stops.

Maria: (*Talking to herself*) What am I doing? I'm going to stand out like a sore thumb. I'm so nervous, I'm going to tip off airport security. How did I talk myself into this? What have I turned into? I can't do this! (*Suddenly she sees John walking into the parking lot toward her.*) John!

EXERCISES FOR SCENE 14

A. What's Going On?
Discuss the following questions with your classmates.

1. How might Maria tell John off?
2. When Maria says, "Actions speak louder than words," what actions is she talking about?
3. What does Maria mean when she says, "It could get pretty ugly"?
4. In what circumstances might Joan step in between Maria and John?
5. How has Joan given Maria the strength to stand alone?
6. What has Maria talked herself into? What has she turned into?
7. What is she going to do?

B. Search Out
Part 1
With a classmate, find and underline 14 phrasal verbs from Scene 14 that begin with the letters S or T and contain one or more of the following particles: in, into, out, on, off, up, down. The verbs are listed in Exercise D, but try to find them first.

Part 2
In the spaces on the next page, list all the phrasal verbs you have underlined. Write "T" next to each transitive verb and write its object. If the phrase includes a pronoun object, write the pronoun between the two parts of the verb. If the phrase is intransitive, write "I" next to it.

1. ___ _____ _____
2. ___ _____ _____
3. ___ _____ _____
4. ___ _____ _____
5. ___ _____ _____
6. ___ _____ _____
7. ___ _____ _____
8. ___ _____ _____
9. ___ _____ _____
10. ___ _____ _____
11. ___ _____ _____
12. ___ _____ _____
13. ___ _____ _____
14. ___ _____ _____

C. Look Back

With a classmate, find three phrasal verbs from Scene 14 with the particles "along," "alone," and "through." Then write your own sentences using the phrasal verbs.

1. _____
   _____
2. _____
   _____
3. _____
   _____

D. Match Up

Match the phrasal verb with the best definition and write the correct letter in the blank.

Part 1

1. take off   _____   a. to anxiously see a situation through to the end
2. think up   _____   b. to yell at someone
3. tell off   _____   c. to become involved
4. take on   _____   d. to leave quickly
5. turn out   _____   e. to happen in a certain way
6. sweat out   _____   f. to accept work or a responsibility
7. step in   _____   g. to come up with an idea

Part 2

8. team up   _____   a. to convince someone not to do something
9. stir up   _____   b. to be easily noticed in a crowd or group by looking or sounding different
10. talk out of   _____   c. to purposefully create trouble or excitement
11. stand out   _____   d. to convince someone to do something
12. tip off   _____   e. to join with another to do something
13. talk into   _____   f. to become someone different than before
14. turn into   _____   g. to give someone secret information

E. Split Up

Fill in the blanks with the correct phrasal verbs from the list below and insert the correct pronoun between the verb and particle. Some verbs require a change in tense.

tell off   sweat out   talk into   tip off   turn into

1. Melanie hates gambling. How did you _____ going to Las Vegas?

2. Susie is a sweet child, but sugary snacks _____ a hyperactive maniac.

3. The next time my sister criticizes me for no good reason, I'm going to _____

   _____.

4. **Daniel:** I wonder what we got on the final exam.

   Rupal: I don't know, but we'll have to _____ until next week when

   the grades come out.

5. When Mrs. Winslow saw her neighbor, Hamid, sneak out of his bedroom window

   at midnight, she called his parents and _____. They were

   waiting for him when he tried to sneak back in at 4:00 a.m.

F. Talk It Over

Discuss the following questions with your classmates.

1. If you saw two people hitting each other in a supermarket, would you step in and break them up? Why or why not?
2. If you drink a lot of alcohol, what kind of person do you turn into?
3. What do you say or do if someone is trying to stir up trouble with you?
4. Have you had to sweat something out at school or work lately? Explain.
5. What unpleasant task or chore have you had to talk yourself into doing? How did you convince yourself to do it?

G. Check-Up

Work with a classmate to fill in the blanks with the correct phrasal verbs from the list below. Some verbs require an object pronoun or a change in tense. Then read the dialogue together.

Part 1

tell off   think up   take off   stand out   team up   turn out

Leroy: So Professor Favoritism gave you a D, too?

Leonard: Yeah, but guess who got a B?

Leroy: Don't tell me. Lisa?

Leonard: You got it. She's his pet. (*Sarcastically*) He wrote that her paper (1)_____ from the rest. But she showed it to me, and mine was a whole lot better than hers. My thesis was clearer, my support was stronger, and my conclusion was more succinct.

Leroy: Are you going to talk to him?

Leonard: I thought we'd better do it together. If we (2)_____, I think our argument will be stronger. But we'd better (3)_____; his office hours end in ten minutes.

Leroy: Have you (4)_____ what you're going to say?

Leonard: I'm going to (5)_____ for giving us D's and threaten to talk to the dean.

Leroy: I don't think things will (6)_____ well if you attack him like that.

Part 2

step in	tip off	talk _ into	talk out of
sweat out	stir up	take on	turn into

Leonard: Don't try and (7)_____ it. I've made up my mind.

Leroy: Well in that case, you can do it alone. Besides, he'll think I'm there to (8)_____ trouble.

Leonard: I'm already as nervous as can be, but you're still going to make me (9)_____ alone!? I can't (10)_____ by myself. I need you there to (11)_____ in case he attacks me. (*Leroy is silent.*) But I don't want to (12)_____ something you don't feel comfortable doing.

Leroy: In that case, I think I'll pass.

Leonard: Well, I've got to run to my car to get my paper. Wish me luck.

Leroy: Good luck. (*When Leonard turns and heads to his car, Leroy* (13)_____ *a snitch and heads to the professor's office to* (14)_____ *about Leonard's plan.*)

H. Make It Up

With a classmate, write a short dialogue in which Francesca gives advice to her daughter, Marina, who feels she's going to stand out because she is very tall for her age. Use at least seven phrasal verbs from Scene 14. When you're finished, read the dialogue to the class.

I. Sum Up and Look Ahead

Briefly summarize what happened in Scene 14. Then ask a classmate what they think will happen between John and Maria in the final scene.

Scene 15: My Love for Him Is All Used Up

Setting Up Scene 15
When Maria sees John, does she still feel a little love for him, or is her love for him all used up?

Pair Up
With a partner, use these phrasal verbs to tell the story of Maria and John.

build up	hold down	stick up for
count on	let down	sort out
fight off	open up	straighten out
give in	put down	stand out
iron out	run out of	use up

My Love for Him Is All Used Up

As John walks across the parking lot, his problems are weighing heavily on him. Suddenly he sees Maria and stops as she stares him down.

John: (*Shocked*) Maria! What are you doing here?!

Maria: (*Sarcastically*) You mean you weren't expecting me to turn up? I'm here to send you off ... (*Maria turns her back on John to reach into her purse. She pulls the pistol out, turns around, and points it at John*) forever! This'll teach you walk out on me!

John: Please don't shoot, Maria! I've left Elaine! I was coming home to you! I'll go back into therapy and work on my problems. We'll work things out together.

Maria: It's a little late for that, isn't it?

John: (*Hoping to wear Maria down with sweet talk*) You're the best thing that ever happened to me. I need you, and you just can't leave me behind. We can still love each other.

Maria: (*She has already written him off and doesn't warm up to him.*) You've used up all my love.

John: (*Changing his tone*) Wise up, Maria, and hand over the gun. (*He walks toward her.*)

Maria: How about a couple of bullets instead? (*As Maria zeroes in on John's heart, Joan rushes up and steps in between them.*)

Joan: Maria! Don't shoot! This is not going to solve anything! It's just going to get you in a worse mess! I've got a good friend who's a great divorce lawyer. Here, give me the gun. Please!

Maria: (*She hesitates before reluctantly handing the gun over to Joan. Looking at John with disgust*) You're right, Joan. He's definitely not worth it. I'm just going to finally wrap up this relationship and get on with my life. (*John, knowing his life has been spared, drops to his knees, tears of relief welling up. Joan and Maria walk off arm in arm, completely ignoring John.*) The gun wasn't loaded, anyway.

EXERCISES: SCENE 15

A. What's Going On?

Discuss the following questions with your classmates.

1. Why does John leave Elaine?
2. Why has Maria already written John off?
3. Is John sincere in wanting to work things out? Explain.
4. Why does Maria zero in on John's heart?
5. Why is John "definitely not worth it"? What does "it" refer to?
6. Would Maria have been justified if she had shot John?
7. Do you think John and Maria will get back together?
8. How did Maria's character change in the last few scenes?
9. Do you feel sorry for John? for Maria? Explain.

B. Search Out

Part 1

With a classmate, find and underline 15 phrasal verbs in Scene 15 that begin with the letters S, T, U, W, or Z and contain one or more of the following particles: in, into, out, on, off, up, down. The verbs are listed in Exercise D, but try to find them first.

Part 2

In the spaces on the next page, list all the phrasal verbs you have underlined. Write "T" next to each transitive verb and write its object. If the phrase includes a pronoun object, write the pronoun between the two parts of the verb. Note that with the three-word verbs, the pronoun follows the verb. If the verb is intransitive, write "I" next to it.

1. ___ _____ _____
2. ___ _____ _____
3. ___ _____ _____
4. ___ _____ _____
5. ___ _____ _____
6. ___ _____ _____
7. ___ _____ _____
8. ___ _____ _____
9. ___ _____ _____
10. ___ _____ _____
11. ___ _____ _____
12. ___ _____ _____
13. ___ _____ _____
14. ___ _____ _____
15. ___ _____ _____

C. Look Back

With a classmate, find three phrasal verbs from Scene 15 with the particles "back," "behind," and "over." Then write your own sentences using the phrasal verbs.

1. _____

_____

2. _____

_____

3. _____

_____

D. Match Up
Match the phrasal verb with the best definition and write the correct letter in the blank.
Part 1

1. stare down   _____   a. to burden or pressure

2. turn up   _____   b. to focus your gaze on someone to make them uncomfortable

3. weigh on   _____   c. to succeed or reach a happy conclusion over time

4. walk out on _____   d. to appear or show up unexpectedly

5. work on   _____   e. to pressure someone to give in

6. work out   _____   f. to try to improve or make something better

7. wear down   _____   g. to leave a spouse suddenly

Part 2

8. write off   _____   a. to realize the truth

9. warm up to   _____   b. to focus on a particular spot

10. use up   _____   c. to bring to a conclusion

11. wise up   _____   d. to exhaust or consume completely

12. zero in on   _____   e. to abandon something or someone as a loss or failure

13. well up   _____   f. to leave someone, often in a rude or angry manner

14. wrap up   _____   g. to begin to feel comfortable with someone or something

15. walk off   _____   h. to build up

E. Split Up
Fill in the blanks with the correct phrasal verbs from the list below and insert the correct pronoun between the verb and particle. Some verbs require a change in tense.

use up   wear down   stare down   write off   work out   wrap up

1. The students kept on talking, so the teacher _____ until they stopped.

2. When a couple is having marital problems, they should go to a therapist to _____.

3. I've had enough of these negotiations. Let's _____ and come to an agreement.

4. Because of the drought, the city has rationed us to 50 gallons of water a day. But by the afternoon, we've _____.

5. Hank refused to answer any questions the first day, but the police kept on asking him questions until they _____ and made him confess to the crime.

6. The poor don't contribute millions of dollars to their campaigns, so the politicians in Washington have _____.

F. Talk It Over
Discuss the following questions with your classmates.

1. What's a good way for a teacher to wrap up a class?
2. Why does a class sometimes never warm up to a teacher?
3. If a child wants to go to the park to play but her parents say no, what can she say or do to wear down her parents until they say yes?
4. What should people do who are trying to work out problems in a relationship?
5. What would you do if a friend turned up unexpectedly at your door for a visit while you were working on an important project?

G. Literal or Figurative?

Fill in the blanks with the correct phrasal verbs from the list below. Some verbs require an object pronoun or a change in tense. Write "F" if the verb is used figuratively and "L" if it's used literally.

weigh on wrap up wear down work on walk off
    write off turn up

____1. Be careful not to _____ the edge of the paper.

____2. My father _____ years ago when, instead of becoming a doctor like him, I chose to be a painter.

____3. That backpack must _____ a lot _____ you.

____4. The thought of my upcoming surgery is starting to _____ me.

____5. The meeting was supposed to end at 6:00 p.m., but they didn't _____ until nearly 9:00.

____6. That box has china in it, so _____ carefully.

____7. I'm sorry, sir, but your car isn't going to pass inspection. Your tires have completely _____.

____8. Working full-time, taking care of three children, and doing four hours of home-work every night has really _____.

____9. When I grow up, I'd like to get a job _____ a farm.

____10. Shelly needs to _____ controlling her temper.

____11. Look both ways before you _____ the sidewalk.

____12. Mariko was so angry, she _____ without saying another word.

____13. The fortune teller told me that when I least expect it, an old friend will _____ _____ on my doorstep.

____14. After you cross West Emerson Street, _____ Myrtle Street.

H. Fill In

Fill in the blanks with the correct phrasal verbs from the list below. Some verbs require an object pronoun or a change in tense.

use up	turn up	stare down	walk out on	warm up to
		wear down	walk off	

1. She may seem like a cold person, but after she gets to know you she'll _____ _____.

2. Before two boxers fight, they try to intimidate each other by _____.

3. In some countries like Brazil, friends don't care if you unexpectedly

   _____.

4. When some students write timed essays, they don't organize their time well, and, therefore, _____ before they can finish.

5. It's really rude to brush someone off by _____ without saying goodbye.

6. I've told my kids we're not going to the beach for summer vacation this year, but they'll try to _____ by bringing it up day after day.

7. Your wife loves you. If you _____, you'll regret it for the rest of your life.

I. Finish Up

Add your own words to complete the sentences.

1. Even though the couple tried to work out their problems, _____

_____

2. If you don't wise up and start to study for the exam, _____

_____

3. He's a great boxer because he can zero in on _____

_____

4. We tried to wrap the meeting up at 8:00 p.m., but _____

_____

5. Because she has so many problems weighing on her, _____

_____

6. I can help you work on your vocabulary _____

_____

7. Not only did his friends write him off, _____

_____

I. Make It Up

With a classmate, write a different ending to the play. When you're finished, read it to the class.

Answer Key

Scene 1: Building Up Anger

B. Search Out, Part 2

1.	T	be (was) up to	no good
2.	I	build up	
3.	T	bring this up	
4.	T	build on	the trust
5.	T	add up to	anything
6.	I	blow up	
7.	T	brush me off	
8.	T	bring out	the worst
9.	T	ask out	every woman
10.	T	back up	your accusations
11.	T	bring it on	
12.	T	believe in	her husband
13.	T	break off	the argument
14.	I	break down	
15.	T	burst into	tears
16.	I	break up	

C. Look Back

1. bounce back   2. answer to

D. Match Up
Part 1   1. f   2. g   3. d   4. b   5. a   6. h   7. c   8. e
Part 2   9. g   10. h   11. f   12. c   13. d   14. e   15. b   16. a

F. Split Up

1. bring it up
2. brushed her off
3. back her up
4. brings it out

5. brings them on
6. ask her out
7. build it up

G. Literal or Figurative?

1. L   build up
2. F   built up
3. F   brought on
4. L   bring on
5. L   build on
6. F   build on
7. F   add up to

8. L   add up to
9. F   bring up
10. L bring them up
11. L burst into
12. F burst into
13. L bring it out
14. F bring out

H. Check-Up
Part 1
1. brought on
2. backing up
3. adds up to
4. brought out
5. brought/up
6. believe in
7. built on

Part 2
8. broke up
9. blew up
10. broke down
11. break/off
12. brushed/off
13. are up to
14. ask/out
15. building up

Scene 2: I Wish I Could Count On You

B. Search Out, Part 2

1.	T	check on	Maria
2.	T	clear up	any doubts
3.	T	catch up on	some accounts
4.	T	come up with	the idea
5.	T	come down with	a cold
6.	T	clean up	my act
7.	T	cut down on	alcohol
8.	T	come on to	me
9.	T	buy into	this story
10.	I	calm down	
11.	T	bail you out	
12.	I	come up	
13.	T	count on	you
14.	T	bring Melissa into	

C. Look Back

1. come between   2. fall behind on

D. Match Up

Part 1	1. c	2. d	3. f	4. a	5. g	6. b	7. e
Part 2	8. e	9. f	10. d	11. a	12. c	13. b	14. g

E. Split Up

1.	cleared it up		4.	clean it up
2.	bail him out		5.	bring him into
3.	calm her down			

G. Literal or Figurative?

1.	L	buy into		8.	F	comes up
2.	F	bought into		9.	L	counts on
3.	L	clear up		10.	F	counted on
4.	F	clear/up		11.	L	catch up
5.	L	bring/into		12.	F	catch up
6.	F	bring/into		13.	F	bailing you out
7.	L	coming up		14.	L	bail him out

Scene3: Fighting Off Something Worse Than a Cold

B. Search Out, Part 2

1.	T	fight off	a cold
2.	T	dump on	you
3.	T	drag you into	
4.	T	fill me in	
5.	T	dream up	the whole thing
6.	T	force herself on	
7.	T	dwell on	the negative
8.	T	dish it out	
9.	T	force it out of	
10.	T	end in	divorce
11.	T	face up to	the fact
12.	T	end up	getting hurt
13.	T	figure out	what to do
14.	T	feel up to	it
15.	T	fill in for	you
16.	I	finish up	

C. Look Back

1. feel for   2. fall apart

D. Match Up

Part 1	1. g	2. c	3. d	4. a	5. b	6. h	7. f	8. e
Part 2	9. f	10. h	11. g	12. e	13. b	14. a	15. d	16. c

F. Split Up

1. force it out
2. dish it out
3. figure him out
4. dreaming it up
5. fight it off
6. fill her in
7. finish it up

G. Literal or Figurative?

1.	L	face up to	9.	L	fight off
2.	F	face up to	10.	F	fight off
3.	L	fill in	11.	F	dump/on
4.	F	fill in	12.	L	dump/on
5.	L	dish out	13.	F	end up
6.	F	dish out	14.	L	ended up
7.	L	force it out of	15.	L	dragged/into
8.	F	force/out of	16.	F	drag/into

Scene4: I Gave In

B. Search Out, Part 2

1.	I	go on	
2.	I	get in	
3.	I	find out	
4.	I	freak out	
5.	T	get into	you
6.	T	get her off	my back
7.	I	give in	
8.	T	gang up on	me
9.	T	go into	it
10.	T	go out with	Elaine

C. Look Back

1. get away with   2. get around

D. Match Up

1. b   2. f   3. e   4. a   5. h   6. i   7. c   8. g   9. j   10. d

F. Finish Up

1. want to go into it
2. to go out with him
3. I give in to them
4. found out/he freaked out
5. didn't get in
6. what got into him/ganging up on him

G. Check-Up

1. getting in
2. going on
3. go into
4. freak out
5. got into

6. ganging up on
7. get off my back
8. go out with
9. find out
10. give in

Scene 5: You Two Will Iron Out Your Differences

B. Search Out, Part 2

1.	T	get me down	
2.	I	give up	
3.	I	go off	
4.	I	foul up	
5.	I	grow up	
6.	T	get on with	my life
7.	T	grow out of	my adolescent ways
8.	I	go on	
9.	T	get out of	another affair
10.	I	hang in	
11.	T	iron out	your differences
12.	T	fix me up	
13.	T	hit it off	

C. Look Back

1. get over
2. get through

D. Match Up

Part 1	1. c	2. g	3. b	4. d	5. f	6. a	7. e
Part 2	8. c	9. b	10. e	11. f	12. a	13. d	

F. Split Up

1. fix me up
2. got him down
3. ironed them out

4. fouled me up
5. gave it up

G. Literal or Figurative?

1.	F	hit it off	8.	L	grow up
2.	L	hit it off	9.	F	grow out of
3.	L	go on	10.	L	grown out of
4.	F	go on	11.	L	got/out of
5.	F	iron them out	12.	F	got/out of
6.	L	iron out	13.	F	go on
7.	F	grow up	14.	L	go on

H. Fill In

1. grow up
2. iron out
3. get on with
4. fix me up/hit it off
5. get/out of
6. give up
7. getting me down/fouled up/hang in
8. go off/go on
9. grow out of it

I. Check-Up

1. going off
2. get me down
3. growing up
4. get/out of
5. go on
6. get on with
7. fixing him up
8. hit it off
9. give up
10. grown out of
11. fouled up
12. iron/out
13. hang in

Scene 6: She Has Trouble Holding Down a Job

B. Search Out, Part 2

1.	T	hold down	a job
2.	I	hold on	
3.	T	knock it off	
4.	T	hear me out	
5.	T	hold up	your refund
6.	T	keep it up	
7.	I	hang up	
8.	T	kiss up to	rude customers
9.	I	lash out	
10.	T	laugh it off	
11.	T	have it out	
12.	I	hang out	
13.	I	hold off	
14.	T	keep out of	other people's affairs
15.	I	heat up	
16.	T	kick out	Bobbi

C. Look Back

1. see to   2. fight back

D Match Up

Part 1	1. h	2. e	3. f	4. g	5. c	6. b	7. a	8. d
Part 2	9. e	10. a	11. c	12. g	13. h	14. b	15. d	16. f

F. Split Up

1.	hold it down	5.	knock it off
2.	kicked her out	6.	held it up
3.	laughed it off	7.	keep it up
4.	hear her out	8.	keep him out

G. Fill In

	Part 1			Part 2
1.	hear me out		8.	lash out
2.	keep it up		9.	laugh it off
3.	holding down		10.	have it out with
4.	hold on		11.	hang out
5.	knock it off		12.	hold off
6.	hold up		13.	kicked them out
7.	kissing up to		14.	keep her out of

Scene 7: You Let Us Down

B. Search Out, Part 2

1.	T	lay you off	
2.	I	look up	
3.	I	let up	
4.	T	live up to	them
5.	T	lead up to	my decision
6.	T	make this up	
7.	T	look into	them
8.	T	look up to	you
9.	T	look down on	you
10.	I	lose out	
11.	T	let us down	
12.	T	look out for	all my employees
13.	T	make me out	
14.	I	mess up	
15.	T	live this down	
16.	T	make it up	
17.	T	make up for	the time
18.	T	live off	my wife's salary

C. Look Back

1. level with   2. make of

D. Match Up

Part 1	1. f	2. e	3. g	4. a	5. d	6. b	7. c	8. i	9. h
Part 2	10. g	11. f	12. c	13. h	14. d	15. b	16. a	17. e	

F. Split Up

1. made it up
2. let us down
3. lays you off
4. mess it up
5. lived it down

H. Messed Up

1. lay me off
2. look down on you
3. look into it
4. let up (take out *my novel*)
5. led up to your
6. messed up badly
7. lose out
8. make up for lost time
9. live up to their dreams
10. let me down
11. made up
12. things are looking up
13. look up to him, too.
14. looks out for her employees
15. live off

I. Check-Up

Part 1

1. looked into
2. messed up
3. live it down
4. led up to
5. let up
6. looking up
7. laid off
8. look out for

Part 2

9. making it up
10. live up to
11. let her down
12. make up for
13. look up to
14. look down on
15. making me out
16. lose out

Scene 8: I Opened Up to You

B. Search Out, Part 2

1.	I	make out	
2.	I	measure up	
3.	T	point out	the fact
4.	T	phase out	my job
5.	I	move on	
6.	T	pick up on	Buddy's nervousness
7.	T	piss me off	
8.	T	pin him down	
9.	T	pass up	the chance
10.	I	move up	
11.	T	mix me up	
12.	I	open up	
13.	T	pour out	my feelings
14.	T	pick on	me
15.	T	own up to	what you did
16.	I	pop out	

C. Look Back

1. cover for   2. pay for

D. Match Up

Part 1 1. g   2. f   3. a   4. h   5. c   6. d   7. b   8. e
Part 2 9. h   10. e   11. a   12. g   13. d   14. f   15. c   16. b

F. Split Up

1. mixing me up   4. pin him down
2. pointed it out   5. pass it up
3. pisses me off   6. move him up

G. Literal or Figurative?

1.	F	pin him down	9.	F	pointed out
2.	L	pinning him down	10.	L	pointed out
3.	F	opening up to	11.	L	poured out
4.	L	opens up to	12.	F	pouring out
5.	L	move on	13.	L	picking on
6.	F	move on	14.	F	picking on
7.	F	mixing me up	15.	F	popped out
8.	L	mix them up	16.	L	popped out

H. Fill In

1. make out
2. pick up on
3. phased out
4. pisses me off
5. point out
6. measure up

I. Messed Up

1. measured up to
2. point out
3. pisses me off
4. move on
5. pin her down
6. move up in/pass it up
7. open up to you
8. pick up on
9. picking on me
10. own up to
11. mixing me up

Scene 9: She Puts Me Down

B. Search Out, Part 2

1. I pile up
2. T put me down
3. T put up with that
4. T put in ten-hour days
5. T put you up to that
6. T put off looking for a new job
7. T put you on
8. T rip off
9. T rub off on me
10. T read up on computer programming
11. T pull that off
12. T rule out counting on his support
13. T rush into anything
14. I pan out

C. Look Back

1. put over
2. plan ahead
3. put away

D. Match Up

Part 1	1. d	2. e	3. g	4. c	5. f	6. a	7. b
Part 2	8. f	9. a	10. g	11. c	12. e	13. d	14. b

F. Split Up

1. put me down
2. putting me on
3. pulled it off

4. rule it out
5. putting it off
6. rip you off

G. Literal or Figurative?

1. F piling up
2. L pile it up
3. L put it down
4. F puts me down
5. F rush into
6. L rushed into
7. L rip it off

8. F ripped me off
9. F rub off on
10. L rub off on
11. L pull him off
12. F pull that off
13. L put in
14. F put in

H. Fill In

1. put in
2. read up on
3. put you up to
4. put off

5. ruled out
6. putting me on
7. put up with

Scene 10: I've Run Out of Patience

B. Search Out, Part 2

1. T run out of   patience
2. T run up against   serious problems
3. T read into   the situation
4. T ride out   the storm
5. I straighten up
6. I stop off
7. T run up   a $1,000 bill
8. I reach out
9. I run into
10. T run out on   you
11. T run off with   her

C. Look Back

1. run away from   2. run to

D. Match Up

1. f   2. c   3. g   4. j   5. d   6. a   7. k   8. h   9. b   10. i   11. e

F. Literal or Figurative?

1.	F	run out of
2.	L	ran out of
3.	L	ran into
4.	F	ran into
5.	F	ran off with
6.	L	run off with
7.	F	reach out
8.	L	reached out
9.	L	straighten up
10.	F	straighten him up
11.	L	run up
12.	F	ran up

G. Fill In

1. run out on
2. stop off
3. ride it out
4. run up against
5. reading into

H. Messed Up

1. run out on
2. ran off with
3. ran into
4. reach out to her
5. ran up a huge bill
6. straighten up
7. ride out the storm
8. run up against
9. reading too much into it
10. run out of time

Scene 11: Stick Up for Yourself

B. Search Out, Part 2

1.	T	rub it in	
2.	T	see in	her
3.	T	see us off	
4.	T	shake up	Maria
5.	I	settle down	
6.	T	settle down with	a nice man
7.	T	spell it out	
8.	I	shape up	
9.	I	ship out	
10.	T	snap out of	it
11.	T	stick up for	yourself
12.	I	show up	
13.	T	stumble on	a great idea
14.	T	settle on	a tiny pistol
15.	T	show off	how well I can shoot

C. Look Back
1. shop around   2. see to   3. get away with

D. Match Up
Part 1   1. f   2. g   3. e   4. c   5. a   6. b   7. d
Part 2   8. a   9. e   10. d   11. h   12. c   13. f   14. b   15. g

F. Split Up
1. see him off
2. shake them up
3. settle her down
4. show it off
5. spell it out
6. shape them up

G. Literal or Figurative?
1. L   stumbled on
2. F   stumbled on
3. F   shook her up
4. L   shake up
5. L   spell it out
6. F   spell it out
7. L   rub it in
8. F   rubbed it in
9. L   see in
10. F   see in him

I. Messed Up
1. snapped out of it
2. see him off
3. spell it out for him
4. shape up or ship out
5. stumbled on
6. stick up for yourself
7. settle down
8. settled on

Scene 12: I Need to Sort a Few Things Out

B. Search Out, Part 2
1. I   start off
2. T   scrape up   enough money
3. I   sink in
4. T   shake off   the realization
5. T   sort out   a few things
6. I   speak up
7. T   set me off
8. I   slow down
9. I   storm off
10. T   shoot off   my mouth

C. Look Back

1.   think over   2.   throw away

D. Match Up

1. f   2. a   3. g   4. d   5. i   6. c   7. b   8. j   9. e   10. h

E. Split Up

1.   shake it off   4.   slowed him down
2.   sets him off   5.   scrape it up
3.   started it off   6.   sort them out

F. Literal or Figurative?

1.   L   shake it off   8.   L   shoot off
2.   F   shake it off   9.   F   sort/out
3.   L   sank in   10.   L   sorted/out
4.   F   sank in   11.   F   scraped up
5.   F   sets me off   12.   L   scape up
6.   L   setting off   13.   L   start off
7.   F   shoot/off   14.   F   start/off

Scene 13: I Straightened Myself Out

B. Search Out, Part 2

1.   T   swear off   this stuff
2.   T   straighten myself out
3.   I   screw up
4.   I   skip off
5.   T   set yourself up
6.   T   take up   time and energy
7.   T   turn off   someone
8.   T   take her out
9.   T   take you up on
10. I   space out
11. I   split up
12. I   sober up
13. T   stay out of   other people's affairs
14. T   take your problems out on
15. I   throw up
16. T   size himself up

C. Look Back
1. turn around   2. hook up with

D. Match Up
Part 1   1. a   2. g   3. b   4. e   5. h   6. f   7. c   8. d
Part 2   9. g   10. a   11. d   12. f   13. b   14. e   15. h   16. c

F. Split Up
1. take them out
2. sober you up
3. set him up
4. screwed it up
5. turned me off
6. split them up
7. straighten him out
8. sizing them up

G. Check Up
Part 1
1. thrown up
2. swore off
3. take him out
4. took them up on
5. straighten out
6. taken up with
7. sober him up

Part 2
8. sized him up
9. split up
10. takes/out on
11. skip off
12. set himself up
13. spaced out
14. stay out of

H. Literal or Figurative?
1. L   set up
2. F   setting yourself up
3. L   split it up
4. F   split up
5. F   straighten out
6. L   straighten them out
7. L   skipped off
8. F   skip off
9. F   turn me off
10. L   turn off
11. L   take it out
12. F   take me out

Scene 14: I'm Going to Stand Out

B. Search Out, Part 2
1. I   take off
2. T   think up   what you're going to say
3. T   tell him off
4. T   take on   all of my problems
5. I   turn out
6. T   sweat this out

7.	I	step in	
8.	I	team up	
9.	T	stir up	trouble
10.	T	talk me out of	seeing this thing through
11.	I	stand out	
12.	T	tip off	security
13.	T	talk myself into	this
14.	I	turn into	

C. Look Back

1. bring along 2. stand alone 3. see through

D. Match Up

Part 1	1. d	2. g	3. b	4. f	5. e	6. a	7. c
Part 2	8. e	9. c	10. a	11. b	12. g	13. d	14. f

E. Split Up

1. talk her into
2. turn her into
3. tell her off
4. sweat it out
5. tipped them off

G. Check Up

Part 1

1. stood out
2. team up
3. take off
4. thought up
5. tell him off
6. turn out

Part 2

7. talk me out of
8. stir up
9. sweat it out
10. take him on
11. step in
12. talk you into
13. turns into
14. tip him off

Scene 15: My Love for Him Is All Used Up

B. Search Out, Part 2

1.	T	weigh on	him
2.	T	stare him down	
3.	I	turn up	
4.	T	walk out on	me
5.	T	work on	my problems
6.	T	work out	things

7.	T	wear down	Maria
8.	T	write him off	
9.	T	warm up to	him
10.	T	use up	all my love
11.	I	wise up	
12.	T	zero in on	John's heart
13.	T	wrap up	this relationship
14.	I	well up	
15.	I	walk off	

C. Look Back

1. go back into
2. leave behind
3. hand over

D. Match Up

Part 1   1. b   2. d   3. a   4. g   5. f   6. c   7. e

Part 2   8. e   9. g   10. d   11. a   12. b   13. h   14. c   15. f

E. Split Up

1. stared them down
2. work them out
3. wrap them up
4. used it up
5. wore him down
6. written them off

G. Literal or Figurative?

1.	L	write off	8.	F	worn me down
2.	F	wrote me off	9.	L	working on
3.	L	weigh/on	10.	F	work on
4.	F	weigh on	11.	L	walk off
5.	F	wrap it up	12.	F	walked off
6.	L	wrap it up	13.	F	turn up
7.	L	worn down	14.	L	turn up

H. Fill In

1. warm up to you
2. staring each other down
3. turn up
4. use their time up
5. walking off
6. wear me down
7. walk out on her

PHRASAL VERB GLOSSARY

<table>
<tr><td>st</td><td>something</td></tr>
<tr><td>sb</td><td>somebody</td></tr>
<tr><td>[t]</td><td>transitive (the verb takes an object)</td></tr>
<tr><td></td><td>Example: Carol asked out Jim.</td></tr>
<tr><td>[i]</td><td>intransitive (the verb doesn't take an object)</td></tr>
<tr><td></td><td>Example: Jim and Mary broke up.</td></tr>
<tr><td>‹ ›</td><td>separable (the object noun can come before or after the particle)</td></tr>
<tr><td></td><td>Example: He brought up the topic.</td></tr>
<tr><td></td><td>He brought the topic up.</td></tr>
</table>

add up to st	[t]	to yield or amount to
answer to sb	[t]	to obey or be obligated to someone
ask sb ‹out›	[t]	to invite someone on a date
back sb/st ‹up›	[t]	to support that what someone is saying
a backup		someone who gives support when needed; a replacement
bail sb ‹out›	[t]	to help someone out of a difficult situation
a bailout		when an organization gives money to another to save it from failure
be up to st	[t]	to be doing something (often something bad)
believe in sb/st	[t]	to have faith or trust in
blow up	[i]	to explode with anger
a blowup		an angry outburst
bounce back	[i]	to return to a previous state of success or health
break down	[i]	to lose control of your emotions
a (nervous) breakdown		when someone becomes mentally ill and can't cope
break st ‹off›	[t]	to suddenly end something

break up	[i]	to end an intimate relationship with someone
a breakup		the end of a relationship
bring sb/st ‹along›	[t]	to take someone or something with one
bring sb/st into st	[t]	to introduce someone or something into a discussion
bring st ‹on›	[t]	to cause something unpleasant to happen
bring st ‹out›	[t]	to elicit or encourage
bring st ‹up›	[t]	to introduce a subject
brush sb ‹off›	[t]	to rudely ignore someone or their ideas
a brush-off		a rude dismissal of someone
build on st	[t]	to use something as a base for further development
build sb/st ‹up›	[t]	to increase gradually
a buildup		a gradual increase
burst into st	[t]	to erupt in (laughter, tears, applause, etc.)
buy into st	[t]	to believe an idea, often a false one
calm down	[i]	to become relaxed after being excited or nervous
catch up on st	[t]	to do work one should have done earlier
check on sb/st	[t]	to find out how or what someone is doing
clean st ‹up›	[t]	to make something or someone become moral or responsible
a cleanup		an act of cleaning
clear st ‹up›	[t]	to help someone understand the facts of a situation
come between sb	[t]	to create trouble between two people
come down with st	[t]	to become ill
come on to sb	[t]	to make clear that one is interested in someone
a come-on		a flirtatious remark or action
come up	[i]	to arise
come up with st	[t]	to think of an idea or plan
count on sb/st	[t]	to depend on or be certain of someone or something
cover for sb	[t]	to help someone avoid trouble by lying for them
cut down on st	[t]	to reduce the amount of something
dish st ‹out›	[t]	to give freely
drag sb into st	[t]	to make someone get involved even if they don't want to
dream st ‹up›	[t]	to think of a plan or idea, especially an unusual one
dump on sb	[t]	to tell someone all of your problems
dwell on st	[t]	to think or talk about something unpleasant for too long
end in st	[t]	to result in
end up	[i]	to come to be in a particular situation without planning it
face up to st	[t]	to accept or acknowledge an unpleasant fact or situation
fall apart	[i]	to have a lot of problems
fall behind on st	[t]	to not do work one should
feel for sb	[t]	to empathize with someone's feelings
feel up to st	[t]	to feel capable or well enough to do something

fight st ‹back›	[t]	to try hard to hide one's feelings
fight sb/st ‹off›	[t]	to try hard to repel or keep away
figure sb/st ‹out›	[t]	to think about something until one understands it
fill sb ‹in›	[t]	to tell someone about recent events they're unaware of
fill in for sb	[t]	to do someone's work
a fill-in		someone or something that temporarily substitutes for another
find out	[i]	to discover or obtain information
finish up	[i]	to complete a task
fix sb ‹up›	[t]	to arrange for two people to meet, usually on a date
force st on sb	[t]	to push on someone something that they don't want
force st out of sb	[t]	to make someone tell something
foul up	[i]	to make a mistake or spoil something
a foul-up		a mistake or a mess caused by a mistake
freak out	[i]	to become very excited or upset
gang up on sb	[t]	to join or work with others against someone
get around st	[t]	to find a way to avoid a problem or obligation
get away with st	[t]	to do something wrong but not get caught or suffer the consequences
get sb down	[i]	to make someone feel unhappy
get in	[i]	to arrive
get into st	[t]	to negatively affect someone's behavior
get sb off sb's back	[t]	to make someone stop annoying or bothering someone
get on with st	[t]	to continue or advance, often after an interruption
get st out of st	[t]	to obtain something beneficial from something or someone
get over st	[t]	to accept a loss or disappointment and resume one's life
get through st	[t]	to work through a problem or difficult situation
give in	[i]	to surrender or yield
give up	[i]	to stop doing, having, or working on something
go back into	[t]	to return to something
go into st	[t]	to explain or discuss in detail
go off	[i]	to leave, often suddenly
go on	[i]	to continue as before
go on	[i]	to happen or take place
go out with sb	[t]	to date someone
grow out of st	[t]	to mature and stop a past behavior
grow up	[i]	to stop acting immature
hand st ‹over›	[t]	to give someone something one is holding
hang in	[i]	to persevere despite difficulties
hang out	[i]	to spend a lot of time somewhere or with someone
a hangout		a place to regularly spend time, often with friends
hang ‹up› st	[t]	to end a phone call
have it out with sb	[t]	to angrily confront someone

hear sb ‹out›	[t]	to listen to someone until they are finished
heat up	[i]	to become more intense
hit it off	[i]	to get along well with someone one just met
hold st ‹down›	[t]	to keep a job
hold st ‹off›	[t]	to postpone
hold on	[i]	to wait for a brief period
hold sb/st ‹up›	[t]	to delay someone or something
a holdup		a delay
hook up with sb	[t]	to meet someone or to become romantically involved with someone
iron st ‹out›	[t]	to solve a problem or difficulty
keep out of st	[t]	to not become involved in a troublesome situation
keep st ‹up›	[t]	to continue or maintain an activity at its current level
kick sb ‹out›	[t]	to force to leave
kiss up to sb	[t]	to try to please someone so they'll do something for one
knock it off	[i]	to stop an annoying behavior
lash out	[i]	to verbally attack someone
laugh st ‹off›	[t]	to ignore or joke about something bothersome
lay sb ‹off›	[t]	to stop employing someone
a layoff		a decision to stop employing someone
lead up to st	[t]	to move toward an important event or decision
leave sb/st ‹behind›	[t]	to choose not to continue with
let sb ‹down›	[t]	to disappoint someone
a letdown		a disappointment
let up	[i]	to decrease or cease
a letup		a decrease in something
level with sb	[t]	to tell someone a difficult truth
live st down	[t]	to overcome the shame of a misdeed or mistake
live off st	[t]	to support oneself
live up to st	[t]	to do as well as expected
look down on sb	[t]	to think one is better than another
look into st	[t]	to try to find out the truth about a problem
look out for sb	[t]	to protect someone's best interests
look up	[i]	to improve
look up to sb	[t]	to admire or respect
lose out	[i]	to not get something one wants
make of st	[t]	to try to understand something confusing
make out	[i]	to succeed or not as a result of effort
make sb/st out	[i]	to create an image
make st ‹up›	[t]	to invent a story or excuse, often to deceive someone
make st ‹up›	[t]	to do something extra to correct something
a makeup		a replacement test for one previously missed

make up for st	[t]	to repay someone
measure up	[i]	to be good enough or meet someone's standards
mess up	[i]	to make a mistake or do something badly
mix sb ‹up›	[t]	to mistake one person or thing for another
a mix-up		a mistake that causes confusion
move on	[i]	to leave a job or situation
move up	[i]	to get a better job or move to a higher level
open up to sb	[t]	to express your feelings or thoughts
own up to st	[t]	to admit to a wrong one has done
pan out	[i]	to develop or happen in a particular way
pass st ‹up›	[t]	to not take advantage of an opportunity or offer
pay for st	[t]	to be punished for a misdeed or mistake
phase st ‹out›	[t]	to gradually stop using or providing something
a phase-out		a gradual move toward stopping something
pick on sb	[t]	to tease or mistreat someone
pick up on st	[t]	to notice or understand something subtle
pile up	[i]	to increase in quantity or amount
a pileup		a collision between a number of cars
pin sb ‹down›	[t]	to make someone commit to or be clear about something
piss sb ‹off›	[t]	to anger
plan ahead	[i]	to prepare for the future
point st/sb ‹out›	[t]	to inform someone of something they didn't know
pop out	[i]	to suddenly say something one hadn't planned to
pour st ‹out›	[t]	to say in a rush, usually something private one has been holding back
pull st ‹off›	[t]	to succeed at a difficult task
put st ‹away›	[t]	to stash away for a future time of need
put sb ‹down›	[t]	to insult or criticize in a mean or cruel way
a put-down		a mean or cruel remark
put st ‹in›	[t]	to spend time or energy doing something or working
put sb/st ‹off›	[t]	to delay or postpone something until a later date
put sb on	[i]	to be untruthful
a put-on		an untrue remark or act to fool someone
put st ‹over›	[t]	to deceive someone
put sb up to st	[t]	to encourage someone to do something
put up with sb/st	[t]	to tolerate
reach out to sb	[t]	to attempt to get closer to someone or to resolve bad feelings
read st into st	[t]	to believe a situation has more importance than it does
read up on st	[t]	to become informed about a subject
ride st ‹out›	[t]	to persevere until a difficult situation has ended
rip sb ‹off›	[t]	to charge more for something than it's worth
a rip-off		the sale of something for a much higher price than it's worth

rub st ‹in›	[t]	to remind someone of something embarrassing to intentionally hurt them
rub off on sb	[t]	to acquire a habit or quality of another person
rule st ‹out›	[t]	to determine something is unlikely or impossible
run away from	[t]	to avoid facing something
run into sb	[t]	to meet someone unexpectantly
run off with sb	[t]	to go away with someone to have an affair
run out of st	[t]	to use up
run out on sb	[t]	to abandon someone
run to sb	[t]	to go to someone with a problem
run st ‹up›	[t]	to accumulate a big debt or to spend a lot of money
run up against sb/st	[t]	to encounter difficult or unexpected problems
rush into st	[t]	to do something suddenly without thinking enough about it
scrape st ‹up›	[t]	to find something scarce, often by being resourceful
screw up	[i]	to mess up or make a mistake
a screwup		a mistake or a person who makes a lot of mistakes
see in sb	[t]	to recognize positive qualities in someone
see sb ‹off›	[t]	to go with someone to a bus, train, or plane terminal to say goodbye
see st ‹through›	[t]	to ensure that something is completed
see to st	[t]	to make sure something will happen
set sb ‹off›	[t]	to annoy
settle down	[i]	to calm down
settle down with	[i]	to establish a home of one's own
settle on st	[t]	to finally decide on something
set sb ‹up›	[t]	to arrange or cause something negative to happen
a setup		an arrangement that leads to negative consequences
shake st ‹off›	[t]	to get rid of a problem or illness
shake sb ‹up›	[t]	to upset or frighten
a shake-up		changes by an organization to make it more effective
shape up	[i]	to improve performance
ship out	[i]	to leave
shoot off sb's mouth	[i]	to say something one shouldn't
shop around	[i]	to go to different places looking for the best thing or price
show off sb/st	[t]	to try to impress people with someone or something
a show-off		a person who tries to impress people
show up	[i]	to arrive
sink in	[i]	to truly understand some information or facts
size sb/st ‹up›	[t]	to make a judgment about a person or situation
skip off	[i]	to leave suddenly and secretly
slow down	[i]	to decrease the rate or speed of something
a slowdown		a decrease in something
snap out of st	[t]	to stop feeling a certain way

sober up	[i]	to gradually become less drunk
sort st ‹out›	[t]	to organize tasks or things that are mixed up
space out	[i]	to lose awareness of one's surroundings and stare off into space
speak up	[i]	to voice your opinion instead of remaining silent
spell st ‹out›	[t]	to explain something clearly
split up	[i]	to end a relationship or marriage
stand alone	[i]	to face a situation without friends or support
stand out	[i]	to be easily noticed in a crowd or group by looking or sounding different
a standout		someone who is easily noticed, usually because they do something very well
stare sb ‹down›	[t]	to focus your gaze on someone to make them uncomfortable
start off	[i]	to begin
stay out of st	[t]	to not get involved
step in	[i]	to become involved
stick up for sb	[t]	to defend
stir st/sb ‹up›	[t]	to purposely create trouble or excitement
stop off	[i]	to make a brief visit
storm off	[i]	to quickly and angrily leave a place or situation
straighten sb/st ‹out›	[t]	to correct improper behavior or work out personal problems
straighten up sb/st	[t]	to correct improper behavior
stumble on st/sb	[t]	to discover something or someone unexpectedly
swear off st	[t]	to promise to stop a certain behavior, usually a negative one
sweat st ‹out›	[t]	to anxiously see a situation through to the end
take off	[i]	to leave quickly
a takeoff		the moment when something leaps into the air
take st ‹on›	[t]	to accept work or a responsibility
take sb ‹out›	[t]	to take someone on a date or pay for an outing
take st out on sb	[t]	to direct anger or frustration with one person or situation against another
take up st	[t]	to fill one's time or space
take sb up on st	[t]	to accept someone's offer
talk sb into st	[t]	to convince someone to do something
talk sb out of st	[t]	to convince someone not to do something
team up	[i]	to join with another to do something
tell sb ‹off›	[t]	to yell at someone
think st ‹over›	[t]	to consider something
think st ‹up›	[t]	to come up with an idea
throw st ‹away›	[t]	to discard or get rid of
throw up	[i]	to bring up food or drink from your stomach
tip sb ‹off›	[t]	to give someone secret information
a tip-off		a warning or a sign that gives something away
turn sb/st ‹around›	[t]	to make a positive change or a bad situation better
turn into	[t]	to become something different than before

turn sb ‹off›	[t]	to lose interest in someone or something
a turnoff		something that makes one lose interest or that disgusts one
turn out	[i]	to happen in a certain way
turn up	[i]	to appear or show up unexpectedly
use st ‹up›	[t]	to exhaust or consume completely
walk off	[i]	to leave someone, often in a rude or angry manner
walk out on sb	[t]	to leave a spouse suddenly
warm up to sb/st	[t]	to begin to feel comfortable with someone or something
a warm-up		something that heats up or prepares something or someone
wear sb ‹down›	[t]	to pressure someone to give in
weigh on sb	[t]	to burden or pressure
well up	[i]	to build up
wise up	[i]	to realize the truth
work on st	[t]	to try to improve or make something better
work st ‹out›	[t]	to succeed or reach a happy conclusion over time
wrap st ‹up›	[t]	to bring to a conclusion
a wrap-up		a report summarizing an event
write sb/st ‹off›	[t]	to abandon something or someone as a loss or failure
a write-off		an elimination of something someone has to pay
zero in on sb/st	[t]	to focus on a particular spot

RECONSTRUCTION

Retell the story using as many phrasal verbs as possible.

Other Books of Interest from Pro Lingua

The Modal Book. This book takes students through the modal verb system and around the world in 14 units that each focus on a different modality and a different country. Students find out what they *should* see, where they *could* go, what they *might* do, and what they *can* and *can't* do in Egypt, India, Thailand, Turkey, and ten other countries. Intermediate and Advanced.

Getting a Fix on Vocabulary. A student text and CD that focus on word-building through affixing prefixes and suffixes and learning common Latin and Greek roots. The vocabulary is presented in the context of fictitious newspaper articles and radio news broadcasts, and practiced in a variety of exercises. Intermediate and Advanced.

Shenanigames. A photocopiable collection of 49 games and activities that cover a wide variety of grammar points. Intermediate and Advanced.

The ESL Miscellany. A copiable teacher resource book of lists that include grammar (all kinds of verbs), 60 vocabulary topics, communicative functions, US and Canadian cultural information, metalinguistic matters, and gestures.

The Idiom Book. A photocopiable text with two CDs. 1010 idioms brought to life in dialogs and exercises in a two-page format. Intermediate and Advanced.

Lexicarry. An all-time best-seller. Over 4500 words and phrases clearly illustrated and keyed to an English word list in the back of the book. Separate word lists are available in ten other languages, including Spanish and Chinese. Multi-level.

The Grammar Review Book. An easy-to-use book designed for learners with inaccurate interlanguage and fossilized errors. Each unit focuses on a problem and leads the students to identify and fix the problem. Intermediate and Advanced.

The Grammar Practice Book. A photocopiable collection of one and two-page individual exercises and pairwork practices. The contents run the gamut of English grammar from basic morphology, phrase structure, and word order to reported speech. Multi-level.

For more information, please visit <u>*ProLinguaLearning.com*</u>.